CU00661933

My New Normal

Surviving My Miscarriages

Lorraine Frederick

ISBN 978-1-64468-872-4 (Paperback)
ISBN 978-1-63630-395-6 (Hardcover)
ISBN 978-1-64468-873-1 (Digital)

Copyright © 2021 Lorraine Frederick
All rights reserved
First Edition

Cover Image Copyright © 2021 by M Moore Studio

All rights reserved. No part of this publication may be reproduced, distributed, or transmitted in any form or by any means, including photocopying, recording, or other electronic or mechanical methods without the prior written permission of the publisher. For permission requests, solicit the publisher via the address below.

Covenant Books, Inc.
11661 Hwy 707
Murrells Inlet, SC 29576
www.covenantbooks.com

Chapter 1

I never thought of my own death the way I thought about it after my third miscarriage, or second for that matter. I imagine everyone thinks of what happens after they die at some point in their life, but this was different. It wasn't this grandiose wonder of what it's like to die or trying to answer the age-old question of what happens and where you go but rather a desire for it. Let's be clear, I would never dream of hurting myself in any way or taking my own life, as I believe that to be the ultimate sin, but it was the first time in my life when death seemed better, or rather easier than living. For the first time I didn't want to live. I felt absolute hopelessness and that I had become a shell of the person I used to be. I felt empty inside, literally and figuratively. I remember moments of holding my belly wishing for my baby to still be there, only to be reminded that they weren't and that I would never have the chance to hold them and whisper the words "I love you," like I had done so many times before in my dreams. I remember having to focus on my husband and parents, my two closest relationships in my life, and think about them and what my death would bring to their lives. It's interesting to me how it's easier for me to be stronger for others than for myself. I guess that is what has made this journey so difficult, so transformative. It changed my life and perspective in ways I could have never imagined.

The ironic thing is that no one talks about miscarriage. When you're younger and thinking about your future, in my case planning my future (I am a planner, also a control freak), I never planned to mourn the death of three unborn babies. There is *so* much out there in society, media, etc. that talks about getting pregnant, being pregnant, having a newborn, and all the trials and tribulations in between becoming a parent. Nothing prepares you for, or even speaks of, when your child dies inside of you. And there is absolutely nothing in this world that can prepare you for that or the first, second, or seventh time you receive a targeted marketing campaign for your baby that's on the way, long after they are gone. I actually remember not wanting to check the mail because I couldn't see another baby offer or coupon from some list I clearly signed up for, let alone find the strength to pull myself out of bed.

I remember thinking about how I felt more prepared than most new parents. I had the privilege of watching my nephew and two nieces being raised and felt I had a better-than-average perspective on what it takes to be a parent, having been exposed to my sister's kids from a very young age. Seeing my godson Julian's terrible twos gave me a preview of what it meant to have a toddler. Seeing Natalia and Gia experience becoming young women has been very meaningful, even when I lived in another state and couldn't see them as often as I would have liked. Given these experiences, I always thought the hard stuff came after the baby was here, or at least on their way with the delivery. It's funny now to think about how nervous the thought of delivery made me before becoming pregnant, now it is the thought of being able to carry full-term that conjure up those same feelings of fear. Ultimately, I felt very alone and isolated through this experience, and sometimes I couldn't find the words to even try to express how I was feeling or the thoughts I was having during the fleeting moments when I even wanted to try to express myself. I was scared to outwardly share the extremely dark thoughts I was having with my husband for fear of how he would handle it. He was grieving too, and the last thing I wanted was to give him reasons to be more concerned about me than he already was. Mostly, I wanted to be alone with my negative thought train and be uninterrupted to delve deeper and deeper into the depression that had consumed me.

This feeling of being alone is what has propelled me to begin writing, while I am still in the midst of the story and the ending is unknown, even to me, the author. Today is October 30, 2019, and I have woken up every day for the last week thinking about starting to write down all of the thoughts I have had, how to begin, and where the story starts. I find myself writing this book in my mind and taking note of all the different emotions, memories, and caveats I want to capture for others to have a window into my experience. My hope is that maybe you find comfort for having some of the same thoughts I had, which at first gave me nothing but more feelings of guilt. There is absolutely nothing worse, than layering feelings of guilt on top of the negative feelings you already have. I started to actually feel bad about feeling bad. There are times when I thought of sharing this nightmare of an experience with others, but only after delivering a healthy child. Sharing this information while I was still in the struggle of despair was never something that crossed my mind, until my friend experienced her first miscarriage.

I was taken aback by her strength and her ability to create a simple post on Facebook less than a week after having a D&C, which was about two weeks ago today. I remember after my D&C feeling like I was in an endless black hole with no desire to get out, let alone make a public proclamation about what I was experiencing. It was much too vulnerable a feeling to share. To see her allow her vulnerability made me feel stronger in some way and also made me relate to her in a way that you can only if you have experienced a miscarriage yourself. A club that no woman wants to be a part of, but here I am. There are no words to say that can capture the emotions experienced, and although I cried the entire time, she inspired me to share a bit of my struggle over the past year and a half publicly. It might seem insignificant, and even feels a little juvenile, to write that an Instagram post was freeing; but it was.

I cannot remember the person, but I recall watching an interview with a well-known entertainer. He talked about his very humble beginnings and how he was self-made with little resources. He made a statement that always stuck with me for whatever reason, and it was something to the extent that it's only cool to share the hard part of your story after you've made it. That no one wants to hear about your struggle while you're still struggling because you haven't done anything with it yet, you haven't overcome the struggle. You're just treading water like everyone else. This statement reminds me of my desire to hold on tight to this silent grief until I was a mother, by society's definition, with a healthy baby in my arms.

That is when it hit me, the correlation between what this person was saying about their struggle and the struggle I still battle today. I needed to feel heard; I needed to relate to someone else. Yet while I endlessly searched for resources or a book to make me feel understood by others that had gone through this, there wasn't really one available that truly spoke to me. This search resulted in me feeling even more alone. I started to feel like waiting to share my experience until I had a healthy child was less authentic, in that I could only share my challenges after having success—a child. My losses are relevant and significant regardless of whether or not my husband and I are able to successfully conceive. I also felt like emptying all the feelings I was experiencing was not only productive and provided a sense of healing for me, but there was potential to help someone else too, someone else that may be looking for the same things I have been searching for, to feel understood, and to be told that it's okay to not be okay.

This feeling of being misunderstood first started when I was provided a handful of five to six books by my therapist. (Yes, I am now seeing a therapist after being diagnosed with postpartum depression from my ob-gyn. More on that later.) I don't mean misunderstood by my therapist. She actually has been a welcomed new element to my life in that she has provided a safe and unbiased third-party perspective for me. She has also made me feel validated. My feelings of isolation were magnified by the books she shared. While some of the books she provided had glimmers of a story I could relate to or emotions I had experienced, I didn't feel like there was anything that really spoke to me, spoke to my soul, and the deepest feelings and thoughts I was having. Thoughts that even now I push out of my head due to fear of manifesting infertility, the thoughts that maybe I will never get the experience of being a mother. In many of the books read, there were many religious undertones. I can certainly understand how religion comes into play when grieving a death, but the last thing I needed was to be told that my heartbreak was part of a bigger plan—even if it was. I am not anti-religious by any means. I grew up Catholic, even went to a Catholic school and wore the uniforms. I have completed my communion, confirmation, and all rituals in between. As I have gotten older, I would consider myself more spiritual than religious. I certainly have a strong independent relationship with God, or a higher power, but the last thing I was searching for were excerpts from the Bible during a time when I needed to have my extremely negative thoughts validated. In some respects, it made me feel worse, in that I was then judging myself for not responding to the words from God, compounding the guilt I was already struggling to release. The cold, harsh reality is that I wasn't in a place to even want to feel better. I was still grieving, and still am, more than a year later. For some strange reason I wanted to hold on to my grief, because in some morbid way it was all I had left of our first child.

I certainly respect others' beliefs; and if turning to God, or the universe, or whatever you call the powers that be can help, then I think that is a beautiful thing. But I wanted to read something that told me I wasn't crazy for not wanting to get out of bed—for days. I wanted to be told that it was normal to feel empty inside, to literally feel hollow, to lose interest in things that normally excited me, to not feel excitement for anything or anyone. To not even want to try to put on a brave face, that you will not smile or laugh for a long time. That those things you once found funny no longer make you bat an eyelash. It felt like I greeted everything and everyone with a blank stare. That it was expected or common to have a decrease in sex drive, because now being intimate with your partner was a thought train that ties sex to pregnancy and ultimately your loss, and there is nothing sexy about that. I desperately wanted to feel normal again, but deep down I knew that I would never be the same person again and that I would have to accept a new normal. That single thought alone was so overwhelming to accept because there were so many unknowns attached to it. Who is the person I am becoming, and will I ever experience true happiness again?

With a few simple but powerful images that spoke to me, I wrote a caption for my public Instagram post that changed my life for the better. Although it was the longest shortest few paragraphs I ever wrote, it felt like an eternity that I sat at my kitchen table and reread the message over and over, each time shedding new tears for my lost babies that I thought I had come to terms with. That's the funny thing about miscarriage—it's grieving a death but also grieving the hopes you had for your child. It's grieving all the looming questions that will forever be unanswered: What will our child look like? What will their personality be like? What will it feel like to finally hold a child of my own? Then, just when you think you have passed the peak of your sadness, you are faced with Mother's Day or your anticipated delivery date and get sucked right back into the darkness. A friend of mine who is grieving a loss recently said to me that the road of grief is not a straight line, and I couldn't have felt those words any more deeply than I did. Just as months and months had passed, and I slowly was able to pick myself up. Something would trigger my sadness, and I would be overcome with the same feelings of despair, only each time they surfaced they became stronger. I often correlate it to being pulled by a riptide. The first pull of the oceans powerful water is undeniable and paralyzing, but each new wave that washes over you feels more intense than the last, until you feel so beaten down that you no longer have the physical strength to swim.

With the time it takes the ultrasound technician to utter the words, "There is no heartbeat," your entire life is turned upside down. Your thoughts change from baby names and nursery-theme planning to disbelief, anger, confusion and what becomes a living nightmare. As soon as my post was published and out there for the world to see, I somehow felt lighter, like a burden had been slightly lifted from my shoulders. Don't get me wrong. I wasn't immediately healed, and all is still not perfect in my world. But then again it never is and never will be. Such is the beauty of life. But I felt joy from this newfound strength and not being afraid for people to know what has been going on in my life, and that was the best I had felt about the events that transpired in a long time. It took a year, but in that moment, I took some of my power back.

The post I published one week ago today accompanied by a few photos that spoke to me read,

I am surprising myself by sharing this publicly, and I think part of this feeling is from the stigma surrounding pregnancy loss. I was inspired by a friend who is grieving her loss to share my story because I know how dark the days surrounding miscarriage can be, and how alone you can feel truly suffering in silence despite those closest to you showing support and love.

My husband and I have lost 3 babies over the last year, and it's been the hardest experience of my entire life. I will never be the person I was before, and I've learned that's ok. There are still bad days, but somehow you push through because honestly you have no other choice. My hope is that by sharing my story and experience, it will not only help me to continue to heal, but for the women reading this that are experiencing it too, to know that you're not alone, this is not your fault, and unfortunately it is much more common than many think. If you're reading this, can relate and it helped you to not feel alone even if only for an instant, sharing this was worth it. #pregnancyandinfantlossawareness #pregnancy-andinfantlossawarenessmonth #1in4

The amount of outreach and positive feedback I received was overwhelming. Many comments echoed the strength I felt to share such an intimate part of my world, condolences, well-wishes, and many private messages from old and current friends. I was humbled by the messages I received from former classmates that had similar experiences. One old friend, who was currently the mother of two beautiful girls, shared that she also had three losses before having her first. She not only offered to recommend fertility doctors she used and experienced success with (actually, the same my husband and I had recently visited), but also shared a few resources with me for support. She shared that the fertility treatments she underwent were the reason for her family. She introduced me to a support group that was by invite only on FB that she was a member of, which was hosted by the fertility office we both visited. She offered to be available to talk with me anytime I needed it and also extended a virtual invitation so I could be added to the closed FB support group. Since that day I have found myself frequenting the online group almost daily to read others' stories and follow along on members' journeys trying to conceive. She shared that she found comfort in reading about others' paths on the road to parenthood, and I was glad to find it did the same for me. I was finally starting to feel less alone, after doing what I thought was the scariest thing. In being open and vulnerable, I found strength. I can't describe the feeling I had when she reached out. It might seem like a small thing, sending a message, but from one woman who has experienced loss to another, in that moment it felt like everything.

A second former classmate reached out to share that she also experienced a loss before having her adorable daughter and son. She said, "You are amazing for speaking up—the stigma/silent grief women experience is terrible. I had one, and in my experience, I found that sometimes when you share, well-meaning people say awful things unintentionally so just wanted to send lots of love your way today." Not only did those words touch my heart. In reading that message, I felt I received some type of personal success as a result of opening up. There have been two large takeaways I have had from this small, but large, experience in sharing a piece of my story publicly. The first is that despite everyone's differences, we are all human having human experiences. I believe that most people on earth have similar life events. They are just experienced at different stages in their journey. I feel that when you are authentic, truly yourself, open and even vulnerable, people respond to it because it's real. It's not the same old thing you see on TV, read in a magazine, or scroll past on social media. We are so inundated with memes and influencers that people don't always share the hurt they have experienced or are currently going through. It's not as cool as to share as your amazing vacation, time out with friends when you look great, or dinner you're having (although I am guilty of posting lots of food too because I am always a foodie at heart). It became part of this realization that by acting in the exact opposite way that I had been, closed off and trying to be independently strong, that I was actually doing myself a disservice. The moment I allowed myself to be vulnerable, I was met with an immediate feeling of strength that was only compounded by the kindness others showed me.

I also had two family members reach out to me. The first shared that she and her husband experienced fertility challenges, failed IVF rounds, and that each of their three children were conceived through IVF. She said, "We know the pain of expecting to hear heartbeats when none were found and all of the doubts that follow. For us it forced difficult conversations that we had not expected to ever have, like are kids a deal breaker? Can we be happy and feel our full worth without them? Is adoption an option? Some answers surprised each other and even ourselves, but in the end, it brought us so much closer. We will never know why things happen the way they do, but we can control the positivity and growth that we draw from each experience." She also provided a fertility doctor referral. What a powerful message to receive, at a time when I was ready to receive it. And that's the kicker. This comes at different moments for everyone. Hopefully, it will be sooner for you than it's been for me. It is no less meaningful regardless of when it comes, but I was so glad to receive her message at a time when I was ready to hear it.

The second relative provided a short but impactful comment on my post that read, "Thank you for sharing...you are such an amazing woman, and you and Kevin are going to make great parents! This was the pick me up I needed for my own miscarriage... Thank you for sharing your strength with us!" Wow, not only did I learn of so many others experiencing this same heartbreak, but it served a purpose. Not only did I find comfort in sharing my story, but it gave others strength too, the same way I found strength in my friend's vulnerability from exposing her truth for all to see. A friend, who recently became a father himself, replied, "You guys will never forget but will love stronger. You guys will be amazing parents when the time comes." He ended his comment with a rainbow emoji, and it wasn't until later that I heard the term *rainbow baby* and realized what it meant.

The Bump, an online source for pregnancy, parenting and baby information defines *rainbow baby* as "a baby that is born shortly after the loss of a previous baby due to miscarriage, stillbirth or death in infancy. This term is given to these special rainbow babies because a rainbow typically follows a storm, giving us hope of what's to come." How beautiful is this sentiment? You can't have a rainbow without the storm. (Random fact: There was a double rainbow at our wedding after a short sprinkle. It made for a beautiful wedding photo, and now I wonder if it was a foreshadowing of what was to come.]

How fitting this part of nature was to this chapter of my life. It is almost like the seasons of New England where I am from and currently reside, how it brings about change every few months, and it is a reminder that nothing is forever or constant. Being in Connecticut in October, Halloween, for that matter today, I can't help but to think about fall as a cycle of death on all hallows eve. I find it interesting that I have found the inspiration to write about my loss during the time of year that is dedicated to remembering the dead. Maybe this book I am writing will be a tactile way that I can remember my babies for years to come. Maybe it will be a reminder of the difficult roads traveled when I am (hopefully) able to find a way to live again one day and no longer feel that I am just existing.

I have always loved this time of year, especially the foliage we see in the northeast. I have fond memories of jumping in big leaf piles raked by my parents. How it always symbolized the beginning of the winter season and the hibernation that's to come. I can't help but feel that fall shows us that there can be beauty in death and can represent both an ending and a new beginning. The leaves turn bright colors of red, yellow, and orange in their final moments before falling to the earth. Ultimately, those leaves become part of the dirt, recycled into the earth. Such is the cycle of life and everything being connected in some way. I certainly have expanded my horizons over the last few years, this past year especially, and have come to believe that every living thing on this earth is connected. I have learned to be quiet, listen, and observe more. It's amazing what you can begin to hear in silence.

Would I have chosen to lose three children in the last twelve months? Absolutely not. But I am still grateful for the time I had with them, even though it was much shorter than I would have ever hoped for. I am grateful for the hope I felt with each baby growing in my womb, sensations I had never experienced, being pregnant, and the miracle that is a woman's body, ever changing with each new day of pregnancy. I still carry the hope with me that I will get to experience bringing a healthy and happy child into our family and the joy of being a mother to a child that was created from the love I share with my husband.

So what is my message here? As tough as it feels, speaking up has potential to make you feel better. This may take a while. I didn't find the courage to open up this way until just last week, and it came from a big push from another person in my life being vulnerable. I couldn't possibly understand more if this is the furthest thing from what you are able to do right now, and that is okay. The biggest message I hope that comes across from reading my story is that it's okay to not be okay. It's okay and absolutely a requirement to give yourself whatever it is that you need. It's okay to feel really bad for days, weeks, months. I know I did. Even if the time is not right now for you, there has to be a time when you start to pick yourself back up but do it when you're ready and not a moment sooner.

To this day, I am grateful for the support my husband gave me during my darkest times. He allowed me the time and space to feel what I was feeling. It was exactly what I needed. As easy as it is to write and much harder to do, try your best to not push away the people in your life who are trying to reach out, especially your partner. You both need each other more than ever right now; you are both grieving an indescribable loss. I do encourage you to voice your needs to those who know what you're going through and never feel bad for setting boundaries or asking for what it is that you need during this time. No one else's feelings, other than your partner's, should be your concern; and anyone that makes you feel otherwise is wrong. It might sound selfish, but I am not sorry. Being selfish was actually not a choice for me. It was what I needed, and I am glad that I didn't feel bad about it. The Lord knows there were plenty of other things in my life to feel bad about at that time.

I think it can be really easy at times to sweep your feelings under the rug and mask that as growth, or acceptance, or moving on. I don't like to make generalizations, but I can speak from my own experience and from speaking with other male friends who have been through a loss or multiple losses with their wives. I sometimes wonder if the loss is harder to process for the fathers or partners. They have to grieve a baby they've never met or felt growing inside of them. Society incorrectly, in my opinion, teaches men from the time they are boys to be strong, don't cry, toughen up when in reality men need to express their emotions too and not feel that it is in anyway a reflection of their masculinity. In my experience, I think I was such a disaster that many times my husband felt the need to be strong for me, when in reality the strongest thing in this moment is to allow your own weakness to show. I spent so much time communicating my feelings that many times he fell silent and listened. Now I certainly needed that, but what was even more helpful was when he shared his feelings with me. His concerns for the future and that it was unknown, concerns that something was "wrong" with one of us, and whether or not we would ever get to experience the joy of being parents. It was these conversations that strengthened our bond, brought us closer, and, most importantly, supported one another and helped to make us not feel alone. As weird as it was, hearing his pain was comforting in a way. It helped me to know that I was not the only one hurting. It allowed me to be strong for him. Of course, deep down I knew he was in pain with me, but I was so consumed with my own feelings that it was sometimes hard to see past my own emotions.

Husbands and partners share the loss of a child with their wives. Although the experience is different, it is no less significant. After sharing my small post and caption, I had a friend reach out to share that he and his wife experienced a loss and what seemed like a long time to conceive. He began his message with a caveat, he said, "Granted I am not a woman, mom, or wife, I can imagine the pain and hurt you must feel. [My wife] and I have been there, she had a miscarriage, and we kept trying forever to get pregnant. Went through all the tests and hoops to figure out why, no answer. Finally, she asked me to come home one night, and before I made it home, I knew she was going to tell me she was pregnant. Now fast forward to seven and a half years later, and if it weren't for the hurt we went through, our son would not have come to us. So, from what you can take from a guy's point of view, you will have your greatest happiness ever after the hurt and loss, you will. God bless." I not only appreciated him reaching out to share his story, but it made me think of my husband even more. To which I replied, "Thank you. I really appreciate you reaching out and sending such a kind message and for sharing your experience. I think a really sad observation I've had is that the guys/dads/husbands aren't acknowledged as much as the woman but they're experiencing the loss too, so just because you're not a woman/mom or wife, it doesn't take away from the hurt I'm sure you felt or make your feelings any less significant. Your son is such a blessing, and I know our day will come, and when it does, we will be so grateful for the opportunity to be parents."

In my quest to find literature that spoke to me during this time, I was extremely saddened to hear multiple stories where marriages did not survive the loss of a child. In those moments of reading other's stories of failed marriages, I was extremely grateful that my husband and I had weathered the storm together, and still are. The thought of potentially losing the most significant person in my life during the absolute worst and hardest time of my life is almost too hurtful a thought to even think, let alone experience. I wanted to take time on this topic because I want to focus on the importance for both partners to lean on each other, regardless of what your relationship looks like. The feeling of a lost child is universal, something we can all relate to regardless if you're the one carrying the child or in other circumstances where you are in the process of adopting or using a surrogate and lose that child before birth. Maybe you are going through the process of IVF, which I myself have not experienced, but I can imagine the roller coaster of hope and disappointment a loss could bring, having so much riding on a single procedure. Each of these circumstances is the same in their significance, disappointment, and impact on your life. Anyone that says otherwise should be avoided during your time of healing. Remember to give yourself what you need, even if that means eliminating some people from your life for the time being, regardless of who they are. You and your spouse come first.

When you are getting married, you have to accept that you don't know everything that the future holds, and that the most important thing is the commitment you are making to each other. You imagine that there are going to be some rough roads ahead to travel and that you may not agree on everything and will have to figure it out, but losing a child isn't something that ever crossed my mind before or after we walked down the aisle. If I am being honest, there is a small part of me that always wondered if I would have trouble getting pregnant, and I am talking from a young age when it was the furthest thing from what I wanted or was ready for or even thinking about for that matter. I always remember my mother talking about how being a mother was the best experience of her life. I saw the joy it brought her, and again when she became a grandmother. Fast forward to the age I am now with many friends having children across a spectrum of ages, with what seems to be a Greater Meriden, Connecticut, baby boom right now, or maybe it's just where my mind is currently focused. For some reason I couldn't see it for myself. I couldn't picture myself being a mom. This was troubling for me, especially after remembering a conversation I had with my husband, where he spoke of being able to picture everything that had transpired in his life to date. That he knew something would happen and come to fruition when he could picture it. I had this looming fear that I would never become a mother because I just couldn't picture it, long before I ever experienced a miscarriage.

Even leading up to getting married and the year after we tied the knot, it was still hard for me to picture myself being a mom even though it was something I knew I wanted. Somehow, even though people do it every day, it felt like a very odd scenario to have another person that was a part of both me and my husband. I wondered if other people had this same idea. Is this a normal thought? I looked forward to parenthood, but it kind of felt like it was not "real life," if that makes sense. How could having an actual child ever be my real life when I couldn't even envision it for myself? Thinking back now, under my new broadened perspective and the belief I have in the power of our internal thoughts, I can't help but wonder if I manifested these tragic events with my worrisome feelings. Or was I insightful and intuitive enough to know what lay ahead?

I remember having a vivid dream after Kevin and I were married, not too long after but certainly before we planned to begin trying to get pregnant. It was the kind of dream that is so vivid that you think it is actually happening, at least that is how it felt. This is now over two years ago, but the feeling is still so strong in my memory. I was sitting on our couch in our living room and was leaning over my newborn baby who was lying on his back looking at me, smiling. I recall this overwhelming feeling of love and joy and fulfillment all at once. Just as I felt my heart couldn't expand any further in that moment, I looked to my left and saw Kevin holding another baby in his arms, proud smile on his face, bouncing the baby up and down as he walked around the kitchen. We had not one but two beautiful babies, twins! As I write about this memory, I am overcome with emotion, tears from remembering the joy I felt, happiness and hope for that dream to become a reality one day. It is everything that I want in this world for myself and my husband, to have a family of our very own.

Sometimes it is very hurtful to feel responsible for what happened. As a woman, there may be times when you think of being pregnant and wonder what it will be like. You know you have a responsibility to make choices for yourself and your baby, but I never anticipated feeling responsible for my baby not making it. I remember from as soon as a few moments after hearing the news to weeks later, I combed through my schedule, from my activities to what I ate, trying to find the cause, only to be left with feelings of guilt and worry. Did I have too hard a workout at kickboxing class? Should I not have done any twists in yoga? Did the glass of wine I had before I knew I was pregnant cause this or maybe the sushi I had before the positive test result? Regardless of my doctor's best efforts to convey that this was in no way my fault and that there was nothing I could have done differently to receive a different outcome, it was not until months later that idea actually resonated and I began to feel less guilt and responsibility for our losses.

The other even less talked about side effect of miscarriage is this feeling of being "less than." At least in my case, I started to feel like less of a woman for not being able to successfully bring a child into the world. I have always been a person that is very confident in who I am. This was instilled in me from a young age. I recall times when I was a kid, I am talking elementary or maybe middle-school aged, where I would come home and criticize my teacher or maybe another adult and how they handled a situation. My mother, trying to be diplomatic, would always listen and encourage me to think for myself. My father who has a "take no shit but do no harm" perspective would egg me on and always reinforced that I should stand up for myself, regardless of my age or who was on the receiving end. To this day I am still grateful for how my parents raised me. To go from this confident little girl to a shell of a woman was quite the transformation. I mean, reproducing is part of my purpose as a woman, right? At least for those that want children, we should be able to bear them. So what was wrong with me, and why wasn't this happening? Why do people that don't even want children get pregnant and give birth so easily? Why are women who are abusing their bodies able to receive this incredible gift while I was willing to do whatever it took to be successful, to only have three back-to-back-to-back failures?

I stood by and watched so many others become pregnant and have a healthy child. While I was genuinely happy for others, it injected more unanswered questions to my negative thought pattern. Was something wrong with me or my husband? Was this happening "for a reason" as they say? I happen to believe in that saying, but I couldn't grasp any reason worthy of this pain. Was the reason that I am not supposed to be a mother? I can be so rigid and judgmental. Maybe I would be too hard on my children. Maybe the universe was saving these babies from an unhappy life and my future bouts of too much discipline and not enough fun? I realize some of these may seem like ridiculous thoughts to think, or maybe you've had a few of them yourself. I know I still do, but now they are less frequent, and I try to be less hard on myself. Now I have learned, and am still learning, to try to combat these negative thoughts with a positive one. The biggest challenge has been, and is, to surrender to what will be. Ultimately, it is out of my hands, and this is a life lesson for a controlling type-A person like myself. I have to trust that the universe is working as it should, and if we are meant to be parents, then we will when the time is right. It's still sad though to think that it may never happen. A thought I am still coming to terms with.

I think part of my fear of sharing our losses with the world was anticipating what people could say. There was a long period of time in between each loss where I had no choice other than to isolate myself for my sake and, to be honest, everyone else's. I have always been known to be outspoken or have trouble holding my tongue. Well, during this time it was amplified. I am so grateful for my husband to this day because he saw parts of me that I didn't even know existed, and he stuck by me during the hardest time of my life when I couldn't even stand myself, all the while he was hurting too.

I remember some of the hurtful comments I had to endure from either well-meaning or ignorant people. I remember being told things like, "At least you know you can get pregnant," "Maybe something was wrong with the baby, and this is why this happened," "You know you've been adding lots of different things into your diet maybe you shouldn't make so many changes next time," "You know there are certain essential oils you can't use when you're pregnant. Maybe you shouldn't use any to avoid a mistake," and the list goes on. I didn't want to go out socially for fear of what others might say, or worse how I might lash out. Yes, I was going to work every day after our first loss and playing that professional role, but being in a personal social setting was much more difficult for me. I would be surrounded by people who knew my struggle, instead of a professional setting where my emotions could be masked by work and deadlines. It was still very difficult to speak about it at the time. I mean, it had been only a few weeks at this point. I remember agonizing over what my response could be to the typical question, "How are you?" I didn't have the strength to put on a fake smile, but I also couldn't be honest, so what do you say? What do you do? I stayed home until I felt like I could answer it. There were times it was unavoidable due to a special event or family/friends get-together, and in those moments, I composed myself as best as I could. Those that knew what was going on understood; and those that didn't, quite frankly, were not my concern. I was in self-preservation mode.

I recall a time shortly after our first loss. It was one of the first nights I mustered up enough energy to leave the house for a social outing. We were out to eat with a group of friends, and one of them made a comment, in an attempt to make light of our situation, with a joke about our loss. It showed such a lack of understanding and empathy that in that moment I did not see, in that moment I was beyond angry. I was stunned. In reflecting today, I have more compassion for those that simply haven't a clue what it means to experience a miscarriage. As I mentioned, we are all humans having human experiences and people make mistakes surely. I know I have. Should I allow one fleeting comment to shape my perception of the entire person? No, I shouldn't. It made me fearful of my relationships in a way. I didn't want to push people away because of how I was feeling, even if they were in the wrong. I simply didn't have the energy for it.

To think this hurtful statement came from one of the people that knew what my husband and I were going through, a friend, a parent at that. I wrongfully assumed that they would know better. No, they hadn't experienced the loss of a child, but they experienced the birth of a child and knew what it meant to bring life to this earth. If a friend could say something hurtful to me, Lord knows what an acquaintance might say. I didn't go out socially for a long time after that night and for good reason. I didn't want to lash out or take my anger out on others, and surely there was enough anger to go around. I was fearful for a long time that I would say something that I couldn't take back and a relationship could be ruined long after I was feeling better. This made me sink deeper into myself and gave me an increased desire to be left alone. I am glad that at that moment I was so in shock from the statement that I was left speechless, something that rarely happens to me. In reflecting on this moment again, it shows how unlike myself I was at that time. Never was I a person to allow someone to speak to me in a way that felt disrespectful, let alone be left with no words to match the circling thoughts in my head. It felt like a breaking point almost, of not only the struggle that had been our life since hearing those fateful words, "There's no heartbeat," but the course my life had been on since moving back to Connecticut after living in New York City for ten years.

I bring up my past in New York for a few reasons. Sharing part of my "before" story I think helps to paint a picture, not only of who I am as a person and who I was but some of the things I have experienced along the way. Most of the experiences I mention pertain to my career, another form of loss I have experienced that has significantly impacted me. More importantly, the connection my career path has to my life now and how different my path is than what I originally envisioned. There is a certain correlation I am now aware of between my own feelings of self-worth and the events that have transpired since 2013 that have shaped the person I am today.

Chapter 2

Thinking of New York City always raises feelings of nostalgia for me. I remember moving there a few short months after graduating high school, ready to take on the city. Many of my classmates thought I was crazy to move to Manhattan at a time when they were looking forward to big campus life and frat parties. I guess, looking back, I always felt a little on the outskirts. I always felt like there were not many people I could really connect with, regardless of the type of relationship, and so many times I was a bit of a loner. A person with lots of acquaintances, but few real friends, this is something I have grown to love as I have gotten older. I now realize the significance of having few meaningful relationships that are sincere than a bunch of people in your social circle that don't have your best interests at heart. I remember coming back to Connecticut to visit for a holiday or long weekend, long after college graduation, when I was officially working in the fashion industry. I was always met with questions about my life in the "big city," and I felt a sense of pride by sharing my experiences. I went to The Fashion Institute of Technology, the school I wanted. In fact, I only applied to one because I was sure that it was the place for me. No backup plan, steadfast that I was going to make it happen. I still remember visiting the campus during their open house and learning that Calvin Klein was an alumnus—*the* Calvin Klein, the designer quoted by Cher in *Clueless*, a cult classic of my childhood. I remember thinking that if one day I could work for Calvin Klein, it would be the most, it would be everything I envisioned for my life at that moment when I was eighteen years young. Clearly, I had a plan.

Sometimes I still wonder if I miss the city (mostly the energy and restaurants, remember I am a foodie) or if I miss the person I was when I moved there. Full of optimism, excitement, a thirst for the future and what it held for me. New experiences to gain, people to meet. A feeling that my life was just beginning in a way. That person is very different than the woman who writes today. I am older, wiser, and, at thirty-four years old, finally understanding the bigger picture. It took a while, and there have been some rough roads traveled for sure, but I am glad I am finally here.

Looking back, I think I was in love with the idea of New York. I had always had an affinity for the city since I was a young child and watched *Who Framed Roger Rabbit* and saw steam coming from sewer grates. Weird but true story, funny to know now as an adult that it was set in Los Angeles. Regardless, New York was a place that seemed foreign and gritty, unlike my home of Meriden, Connecticut. Although I always thought I grew up in a city, I realized it was nowhere near the scale of where I envisioned myself being after seeing NYC in the movies and finally in real life in my teens. For some reason it was a place I always saw myself living, a place that could deliver on the high aspirations I had for myself, back when I equated success with status and materialistic things. Sure, it felt great to say I worked for Calvin Klein, the last job I had before moving back to Connecticut, but this was a tumultuous time of finding myself, struggling to make it and survive in the city. On the outside I appeared happy and projected, that I had it together. In truth, it was a time when I was questioning my life choices and whether I would ever find true happiness. If I wasn't feeling fulfillment at my dream job in my dream city in my very own apartment in Manhattan, then what exactly was missing?

These questions raise this idea for me of the difference between perception and reality. I believe that reality is a perception. Actually, each person's perception is their own reality. I was confident, had goals I was realizing, and that did bring a level of joy; but I was never fulfilled. I was in my twenties, and so it was easy to be blinded by the glitz of the city and the opportunities and experiences it brings. Don't get me wrong, I met some great people and had "once in a lifetime" experiences but at the end of the day it didn't really matter.

It didn't really matter to me anymore because it felt so superficial. I no longer cared about trivial things like designer shoes and eating at the newest restaurant (well, less about the restaurants). I was longing for something more significant, more meaningful for me at that time in my life.

I had the luxury of being introduced to my husband through mutual friends. I was doing well in the city professionally, had experienced two promotions within a four-year span, and had my eyes on making the switch to another division with my company, an opportunity that would let me realize the goal I set during that fateful open house at FIT, to work for the Calvin Klein brand. It was around this time, where I had a conversation with my now husband, that I will never forget. It made me see him for who he really is and made me understand what was missing in my life all at the same time. He had left Connecticut to attend Marist College in Poughkeepsie and lived in New York for four years before returning home to work in Connecticut, a similar but different path than mine. While I never envisioned myself living in New York forever, I wasn't sure I would move back to my hometown but definitely my home state was an attractive option. I asked him if he ever felt a desire to leave our hometown of Meriden and experience living and working full time in another location or go back to New York for that matter. His response is something I will never forget. With the most sincerity, he said he felt it was important that some people stay in their hometown, to help give back to the community you are from and make it better for future generations. I knew I already cared for him well before this conversation, but I found a new level of respect and admiration for him after he shared this. It told me a lot about the type of person he was and the type of person I wanted to be. It felt like in that moment I realized what was missing in my life, and that was pursuing work that helped other people, truly a feeling of fulfillment I hadn't experienced. It also brought up something in me that deep down I knew was already there, a different perspective that was a direct contradiction to the life I was living.

It was around this time when I accepted my new role as national public relations and marketing manager for Calvin Klein jeans and underwear. Two weeks after I accepted the job offer, it was announced that my company, who owned the rights to the jeans and underwear business, was being acquired by PVH, the parent company of Calvin Klein Inc. This was certainly not part of my plan. It was a time of uncertainty and clarity—uncertainty about how the new role would unfold given the business merger, uncertainty for what my next goal was now that I had achieved one from nine years prior, and clarity that I wanted to pursue my new relationship with the hope that it would become something more. Seven months after my now-husband Kevin and I began dating, seven months into my dream job, I quit, packed my bags for Connecticut, and moved in with Kevin. I never looked back. I remember being so uncertain about what my career path would look like outside of the city, but ultimately, it didn't matter to me at that point because I was certain about my personal relationship and where I knew my life was going. I envisioned and longed for us to build a life together and ultimately start our family, something I felt was now on the horizon and part of my new plan. I remember at that time, and still to this day, loving seeing Kevin in his element as a special education teacher. To see him with children somehow made him more attractive. It also allowed me to envision the type of father he could be, despite my own inability to envision parenthood for myself.

I was thrilled when I landed a job in Stamford for a global baby furniture company. It was more responsibility and a pay increase, something I was not anticipating leaving the city, an added bonus with the lower cost of living in Connecticut. The high was short-lived when I was let go from the role, the first time I had ever been dismissed from a job and unfortunately not the last. I worked for this company from May until August, too short to make an impact, but quick enough to make an impression. I didn't see eye to eye with my supervisor, the president of the North American business, and couldn't help but to point out that the idea I had proposed weeks prior that she dismissed as absurd was being implemented by head-quarters in Norway. Remember that outspoken character trait I mentioned earlier? Remember that little girl being egged on by her father to speak up? Well, I probably shouldn't have listened to that inner

25

voice, but I did. I believe it is what sealed my fate, but ultimately, it was for the better. This was the first time my ego took a significant hit and the first time I began to question my own identity, a theme that continued to resurface for years to come.

It's funny how long I have relied on the saying that "everything happens for a reason." As cliché as it sounds, I always felt this to be true. As true as I still believe it is to this very day. It was not until this past year that I started living by that saying and not just believing it. In hindsight it is always easier to be objective, and this is still something I struggle with for our losses. Although I can rationalize that there are many things that would have not happened in our lives had our babies been born full term, it is a big pill to swallow that there is any reason good enough to have to mourn your own child.

I was unemployed; lived back in my hometown; and it was August of 2013, the start of football season. Normally, football season wouldn't have any significance in my story. But you see, my husband is a football coach; and so at a time when I was envisioning us creating a life together, me finding my way in Connecticut, picking up old friendships where they left off, and figuring out the rest along the way, I found myself depressed, uncertain, and alone a lot of the time. It was a difficult transition to say the least. My confidence had taken a big hit. Sometimes I felt resentment for leaving a life I had built in New York, only to remind myself that I was not only accountable for that decision but the truth was I hadn't been happy in New York for some time and Kevin wasn't responsible for my happiness, or unhappiness for that matter. I was left with this curiosity of what I was meant to do and the task of building my confidence back up after being professionally rejected. Being released from your job can almost be described as an unwanted breakup, where you're blindsided and still want to make it work. I had always received such positive feedback from employers, and so it was a big shock to say the least. My plan was on hold for the time being.

I ended up taking a job with a digital advertising company in Middletown not far from home in January 2014. It was a project manager role for one of the employees that was going on maternity leave. It wasn't marketing, which was where my passion lay, but it was an opportunity to have a reason to get out of bed in the morning, something I desperately needed after being unemployed for several months. I lasted three months before taking a job with a former boss of mine that I worked for years ago in a hair salon. She had since added a cosmetology school to her list of businesses. I felt excited for a job opportunity, something that I hadn't felt since being offered that first job in Stamford when I was planning my move back to Connecticut. It wasn't the fashion industry, and that certainly was not a requirement, but the beauty industry felt like a distant cousin of the world I was so used to being in. I was sold a picture-perfect position that left many details out. Within a few short months, I felt overworked, underappreciated, and definitely underpaid. It was the second pay cut I had taken since relocating, and that coupled with the schedule and unrealistic expectations left much to be desired. I worked long hours, and it began to take a toll on me. I was looking for a new job within a few months. I stayed with the cosmetology school for what seemed like an eternity but was, in fact, a year and seven months. Providing my resignation that day, well, I hadn't been that certain about anything since leaving New York two years earlier. My plan felt like it was starting to take shape again, and I felt a boost in confidence that was finally a nod to my old self.

I was excited to accept a role at a small privately-owned company that specialized in artisan gifts. It was an opportunity to get back into the consumer packaged goods (CPG) space and work on marketing campaigns, something I was beginning to miss. Over the next two and a half years, I learned a lot about myself. I got engaged and married. At work I was put in tough positions, had managers who were uneducated in what my role was or should be, and so it was never the right fit. I was often left wondering if I was losing my mind after leaving meetings that had no purpose or did not make sense, where management did not lead and took credit for other's ideas. At one point I was actually told that when I was hired two years prior, they were in fact looking for a different skill set but now saw value in my experience. Two years of hard work I had given before they saw my value. The ironic thing is, somehow, they felt this was a positive they were sharing with me. To be told by the CEO that they in fact didn't see my value until after being there for two years was all I needed to hear to start looking for another job. I was let go before I found another opportunity, and so here I was, unemployed again. I was fortunate to make a few friends there that kept me sane during that crazy time, and I am grateful that I am still in touch with the two I counted on most. Life is funny that way. Sometimes it's hard to see purpose in an experience. When I was let go from my position that fateful day, I knew the purpose of that business had been served for me, in making introductions for friends that I believe I will have for a lifetime.

Back to square one, unemployed for the second time. I remember thinking, *Now what do I do?* This time I was a newlywed, quickly approaching our one-year anniversary, and I felt like a failure despite having many positives in my life, including a new husband and a home to call our own. That is the thing about relationships. It is the one that you have with yourself that matters most, and I was battling another hit to my confidence, was even questioning who I was. In reflecting back, I may have put too much pressure on Kevin to provide happiness for me instead of doing it for myself, a theme I now have the luxury of seeing through my writing. I read something the other day that I thought was beautiful, two things actually. The first was, "Make sure your cup is full first, you can't pour from an empty cup," and the second was, "You don't need someone to complete you, you only need them to accept you completely." I think it's easy to see why they both resonate with me now. I needed to fill my cup these last twelve months, and I still am. I also need to continue to work on my own happiness so that I can bring that inner joy to my marriage.

Despite the house we had purchased together a few years back and finding a job that I thought I could make work, not to mention lost and changed friendships and a strained relationship with my sister, things sure looked a lot different than the picture I had painted for myself while I lived in New York and daydreamed about moving back to Meriden five years earlier. There were times that the realization that things were not as I had hoped for them to be really brought me down. I wasn't working, and so I was convinced that we couldn't begin our journey to start a family. It felt irresponsible to me to actively bring a child into the world when I didn't feel financially stable with a stable income. It reminds me of the quote from a John Lennon song, "Life is what happens to you while you're busy making plans," something a control freak like myself has had a really hard time accepting. That is the reality of life. You can't plan everything. As much I still try, I fear this will be a lifelong lesson that I am still learning. The past year and a few months have definitely propelled some unwanted growth. I even remember thinking that these losses were my first lesson in parenthood, that it was some sick joke to get me to understand that things are out of my hands, and that I have to learn to let go and go with the flow. I am still holding on a bit.

For as long as I can remember I have always been very goal oriented, very task focused. For some reason, accomplishing things on a to-do list brings me joy or maybe the feeling of being productive and moving forward (or maybe it just gives me a false sense of control). I will even admit to adding things to my to-do list that I have already done just so I can cross them off. (Yes, I still do this. In fact, I did it last week.) What is it about this drive that makes me feel guilty for staying still? Like I am failing if I am not moving forward or working toward the next goal. In sitting here writing in an attempt to try to catch up to the thoughts that are pouring out of me, I know now that part of my struggle with our three losses was not only a desire to remain still but a need to do so. I think even in my grief I felt guilty for giving myself what I needed. The shoulds kept coming and going like waves in the ocean of my brain: I should be getting up, I should try to accomplish something today, I should make my husband dinner even though I hadn't had an appetite for days, but the reality is that I could not.

Sometimes I could not muster up the courage to call my mother to say hello because I couldn't bear the thought of her bringing up the baby or her desire for another grandchild. She was excited at the thought of Kevin and I becoming parents and sharing that joy with us but had no idea how much pain it brought me to have this part of our discussions at that time, and even sometimes still to this day. Other times it's all I wanted to talk about, sometimes bringing it up to Kevin when I am sure he needed a break from it all too. What I am working on today, and have been for some time, is giving myself a break and I mean a *real break*. Not beating myself up if I accomplished 75 percent of my list or 50 percent or 10 percent for that matter. In fact, I haven't written a list since last week. (Remember the list where I added two things that I had already done.) I have been sleeping later and feeling more lethargic. Maybe that is a sign that my depressive state is on its way back, or maybe it was resurfaced from my friend's loss. Maybe it's simply emotions that are coming about knowing that I am ovulating next week and it's the first time in the last two months that we can try again, though I am not certain I am ready.

Who knows, maybe it's a combination of all three. Maybe I am still grieving the third child we lost on August 4, 2019. I was just over six weeks along. I am learning to give myself what I need, regardless of how that changes day to day, and what I need most is to love myself and stop being so judgmental of how I am feeling or what I desire. It's okay to not be okay, and I am still not all the way okay.

I remember dreaming big at FIT, initially thinking I would be a designer and boutique owner, before a close call with a shoe sander in my accessories-design class made me realize it wasn't something I saw myself doing for a lifetime. I went back to marketing, something I always enjoyed and felt came naturally to me. I envisioned one day being a chief marketing officer for a large well-known brand and sailing off into the sunset, or maybe a penthouse. On the road to being a CMO was my goal of being a director of marketing. As I recalled these aspirations, I thought to myself that surely my years and breadth of experience to date has prepared me for that responsibility. It was a matter of finding a company that agreed and could provide a real chance for growth in a new place to call home.

This second time around I was unemployed during the month of June and July of 2018, not bad months to be out of work in New England. To add, with my husband being a teacher, we got to spend some good quality time. Even though I secretly worried about my next career move deep down, I didn't show it. It was an exciting time in that my brother-in-law was engaged and we were hosting their engagement party at our home. I had the time and energy to do some work in our home in preparations for the party, and it was a welcomed distraction from my lack of employment or triggers that brought on my postpartum depression. On a whim I applied to a director of marketing role I saw for a company I hadn't heard of but was only twenty minutes away from home. It felt too good to be true. I remember the interview and receiving the job offer the same day. I was thrilled. I was taking a step ahead in terms of my title, reaching that goal of being a director of marketing, not to mention some plush benefits in terms of salary and my new office. It felt like everything was coming together, finally.

My husband and I had just celebrated our one-year wedding anniversary, and talks to start a family became more common now that our first year we wanted to enjoy together as newlyweds had come to an end. My age started to become a factor, being thirty-three at the time, but I had concern for trying to get pregnant so soon after starting a new job. I felt a strong sense of responsibility, was hiring a team, and was taking on the type of role I had desired for a long time with what I believed included autonomy. Within a few weeks, I had confirmed travel to Las Vegas for a trade show and Dubai (yes, Dubai!) for customer meetings. These two trips were followed by a weekend in Chicago to attend an executive education program hosted by Columbia University and Google. I was riding high for sure, and it was easy to see then why my last job didn't work out, because this opportunity was waiting for me. Unfortunately, I can never justify our losses with this same rationale, because even if we are lucky enough to have a baby earth side one day, it will never replace the three we've lost. There will always be a sadness I carry with me in remembering them.

Despite my initial concern with getting pregnant so soon after starting a new job, my husband and I decided that life shouldn't wait for circumstance and so we forged ahead with our first attempt to get pregnant. It was July 2018 when I stopped taking my birth control, August when I started the job, and the end of August when I confirmed my first pregnancy. I remember it being a strange few weeks filled with uncertainty and change. We weren't expecting to get pregnant so fast, and it was so quick that once it was confirmed, I questioned if I was ready for all of the changes that were now clearly ahead. Although, in speaking to every parent on the face of the earth, apparently you are never really ready. I was certain I was pregnant when I missed my period in August and baffled when the test came back negative. It was odd because, although I had never been pregnant before and so I couldn't be sure what it felt like, I was pretty positive I was.

I remember talking with a friend who shared that after she stopped taking birth control a few years back, she didn't get her period for a few months, something that apparently is not that uncommon. And so I chalked it up to my body adjusting from not being on the pill and went on my merry way. Another week passed and then another, and something was nagging at me to take another test. When I did, there it was—the positive result I had been sure of from the start. I blurted it out to Kevin because I was both shocked and excited. His face said he was feeling the same. No time for cute announcements to make the moment special, just an "I'm pregnant" while holding the test in hand in the kitchen on a Tuesday. Although I took a few more with all the same result, we scheduled an appointment with the doctor to be sure.

Within the week we waited for our first appointment, our excitement began to grow. I would read daily messages aloud each night after dinner from an app that compared the size of the baby to some type of food item or detailed what parts of their body was growing. The following week the doctor confirmed what I already knew, and then we let ourselves really get excited. The following four weeks included us having our parents over for dinner where we shared the news with books on "how to be a grandpa" for our dads and similar books for grandmas for our moms. Our mothers shed tears of joy. We each called our siblings to share the news. Although it was early, we wanted to share our happiness with our immediate family. My husband and I were so excited we even shared the news with a few close friends. If I am being honest, it was hard to keep it a secret even the first time hanging out socially and not indulging in a glass of wine (especially for those that knew we were trying to get pregnant).

It was Monday, September 17, 2018. I was nine weeks pregnant. I had just gotten back from my first work trip to Las Vegas at my new job. I had posted a photo of myself at the convention where I am still convinced you can see my baby bump, even if invisible to the naked eye. Maybe it was just that I knew they were there and that my skinny jeans were feeling extra tight, but even now when I look at the image, I see the roundness of my belly. At the time I didn't know that it would be the only memory of this pregnancy I would ever have. A week prior I had gone in for my first ultrasound. My husband and I waited anxiously to see exactly how far along we were and to hear the heartbeat for the first time. As a result of me getting pregnant right away after stopping my birth control and not having a cycle in between stopping the pill and getting pregnant, my doctor shared it was tough to know exactly how far along I was but that the ultrasound could help with that. On that day, there was no heartbeat. Not all hope was gone, according to the doctor, even though deep down I knew I had lost the baby. She prepared us for the worst but also said that we should come back in one more week to have another ultrasound. Maybe I wasn't as far along as she thought and it was too soon to hear the heart. She did emphasize that while there was still a chance for a full-term baby, if we didn't hear a heartbeat in a week, we could be certain that the pregnancy was not viable.

Not viable? Was that the best way to communicate the worst news an expecting couple could hear? If I am being honest, she was kind at that moment but I was angry, sad, confused, and inconsolable. The following week was a blur. I had a strict vacation schedule at my new job and was left with no option but to tell my boss that I was pregnant and had to have doctor's appointments during working hours. I was happily surprised at how understanding he was, and I wonder if him becoming a father for the first time the year prior helped with that. I was delighted to even receive an e-mail of well-wishes from the CEO, something that was out of his character according to the long-term employees. I explained that I had to go to another ultrasound the following week. My trip to Las Vegas fell in between my first ultrasound and the second that we were desperately awaiting, and so I tried to focus on my work ahead and everything that had to be completed before getting on that plane.

To this day I haven't shared with Kevin that I cried in the shower every day that week. He was trying to be optimistic, but something deep inside of me knew it was over, but I couldn't bear the news. I wanted to be strong for him and not show that I had lost hope. I remember him asking me if I still felt pregnant, which I sometimes thought I did, and other times wasn't sure. I remember my hand always finding its way to my belly, trying to provide extra support for the life that was there. I had never been pregnant before, and I'd never had a miscarriage, so there was no way to be sure. I wasn't showing any physical signs of miscarriage, and so I held on to that fact as a small glimmer of hope. I told myself to keep it together and get through this trip so that I could get to the next ultrasound appointment and have them tell me everything was okay.

The day came and went. I recall crying in the general waiting area after the ultrasound. The technician escorted us back out after confirming there was no heartbeat and no growth since our last visit a week earlier. Her cold words and nonchalant bedside manner are still with me to this day. I am sure this was not the first or last time she had to deliver those words, but I believe that compassion is a trait that should be required for certain professions, hers included. I had barely gotten dressed and was keeled over with my head resting against the wall behind the drawn curtain for me to change. I was in shock but also was waiting for this news in a way. I recall feeling rushed to leave the room, something that felt very cold after receiving such a devastating blow. I was in too much despair to put up a fight. I remember not caring that I was crying in public, while other pregnant women, *visibly pregnant women*, awaited their appointments in the waiting room or how grateful I was when Kevin demanded that we receive a private room to wait for the doctor so that we could have some privacy to try to absorb the news we had just received. I know the next thirty minutes were filled with tears, condolences, and bouts of optimism from Kevin; but I felt numb. It's a strange feeling to carry a child that you're told is no longer living. I felt an instant instinct to defend myself and my unborn child that rushed to the surface, and I was in utter disbelief and didn't want to believe what they were saying was true. I had the desire for the connection with my child to not end, but also the morbid thought that life is no longer inside of me. Now I am just carrying my babies body. I didn't want to believe it, and with certainty even told my husband that I thought they made a mistake. I mean, doctors make mistakes too, right?

I texted my boss to alert him of the news, certain that he would tell me to take the rest of the day off. Boy, was I wrong. I remember Kevin being so angry that I had to go back to work and I felt both surprised, but more so defeated. I've lost our baby; I can't lose this job too. What an incredible amount of pressure I unfairly put on myself. The person so laser focused on what needs to be done and the next goal to reach that I am not only missing what's right in front of me, but also was not giving myself what I really needed. Making time for myself, being easier on myself, and slowing down are all things that I have been working on. It hasn't been easy, but it is most certainly worth it.

For days I was certain they made a mistake. I spent countless hours on the Internet finding story after story of no heartbeat until twelve, thirteen, fourteen weeks. I was determined to prove the doctor wrong. I had not one symptom of miscarriage. I still looked pregnant. My nipples still felt sore under the hot water of a morning shower. I still felt exhausted. It was during this time that I learned what a "missed miscarriage" is. It is a loss without any of the symptoms you would expect or at least imagine. I didn't lose the baby at home. In fact, my body never recognized the loss, and so I was left in this in-between phase of having to make a choice of how to proceed. It was a far cry from thinking about what names to pick or color to paint the nursery. Now I was faced with three options: (1) Do nothing and wait for nature to take its course, (2) Take a pill that would set my body into labor so I could miscarry at home, or (3) Have a D&C procedure where the baby is surgically removed. As these options were shared with me, I was still in a state of shock. It was maybe forty minutes after receiving the news that our baby was gone. It was positioned to me that it was not recommended to wait for nature because there was no sense of when or where it could start, which could pose a real issue for a working woman. The second option of taking a pill to induce the loss provided the comfort of home and a somewhat controlled time frame, but no certainty that I wouldn't still require a D&C if the miscarriage was incomplete. Given my upcoming work travel at the time to Dubai for a week in a week, I opted for the D&C, hoping for a more seamless experience and wanting this portion of the nightmare to be over.

Kevin and my mother were there with me that day. I remember cracking jokes to lighten the mood. Something I have become more aware of myself lately is that it seems it is harder for me to see others uncomfortable or feel pain than to feel it myself and so I deflected at a time when all I wanted to do was cry. I made jokes to distract them and myself from what was about to happen to my body and my baby. I don't even remember going home that day, but I do remember going to work the following day. HR stopped into my office, who was aware of what was happening, and asked why I didn't take a day at home. I had even gone into work the morning of the procedure. I don't know if it was more my need for a distraction or the desire to prove how committed I was to my job that drove me there. Professional women in this position, or any working mother for that matter, can understand the added pressures that women face by employers. Nothing is said, but there is always an underlying feeling that as a woman you cannot show any vulnerability or admit that you are experiencing hormonal roller coasters despite the fact that every human being can acknowledge that women's bodies do amazing things, including having a baby. We just aren't allowed to show any negative consequences as a result of the process. Sure, there are laws to provide some protection, but the reality is that needing time for a personal or family problem can be a negative reflection, even for the women who worked the day of and after her D&C. After the procedure, it was shared with me that I might experience period-like symptoms following the surgery, with one large caveat: given the procedure, I was not able to use tampons.

Fast forward to a week later, and I am on a thirteen-hour flight to Dubai wearing what felt like a diaper. I traveled to a destination

I had always dreamt of visiting, but it was during the worst part of my life until that point. I drowned my sorrows in afternoon cocktails by the pool that I couldn't enjoy in one-hundred-degree weather. I focused on the upcoming meetings and took in a few sights, anything to distract from the thoughts in my brain.

We had the chance to visit the Dubai mall, and I remember strolling through the upscale department stores, finding my way to a small jewelry section that featured beautiful handmade rings, earrings, and necklaces. I had never heard of the designer but found myself drawn to this particular jewelry display. I left without purchasing myself anything, even though I really loved two stacking rings in particular. I found myself thinking of the rings later that day in my hotel room, and even the following day when I was preparing for our upcoming client meetings. Something pushed me to go back to the mall the next day, and I decided to purchase the rings. They were a few hundred dollars that I felt I shouldn't spend, but considering it would be a nice memento of the trip, I thought a little retail therapy wasn't the worst thing for me at the time. It wasn't until later that I researched the meaning of the blue lace agate stone featured in both rings that I realized why I was so drawn to them. In reading about the stone's properties online, it stated that blue lace agate is a warm stone with protective properties, encouraging security and self-confidence. It went on to say that it was a great stone to use during pregnancy and that it helps new mothers avoid the baby blues sometimes experienced after giving birth. I cried when reading this in my hotel room. It felt like my child had led me to the rings in a way, that the baby wanted me to feel supported. The baby knew I needed to be lifted up in my sorrow, and I felt a sense of comfort from wearing them. They became a symbol and reminder of my first pregnancy, and I have not taken the rings off since that day.

In a way it was refreshing to have a change of scenery and some distractions during that time, but it was only a matter of time before I had to head home and face reality. I remember tears immediately streaming down my cheeks uncontrollably as soon as we landed at JFK. It wasn't home, but it was as close to home as I had been in the past week, and my emotions came like a tidal wave that washed over me. I somehow composed myself before meeting up with my boss and colleague for the four plus hours it took us to get home. It felt like the car ride would never end.

The holidays were especially tough. It was a time I had been looking forward to. By that time I would be far enough along that it would be "safe" to share the news with extended family, but we no longer had that news to share. I buried myself in my work while I was trying to come to sorts with what had transpired, trying to make sense of it all. I certainly was not ready to try to get pregnant again and needed time, but there was also that nagging feeling of time slipping away and potentially more complications becoming present as I got older. As my thirty-fourth birthday approached last January, I was starting to feel a little bit like myself. I was convinced that our first experience being pregnant was a fluke and that we would put this experience behind us so that we could move forward. I had feelings of guilt for wanting to try again and also for starting to feel like myself again. Part of me wanted to remain in this deep depression because it was the only thing that linked me to my baby. In a way, it felt like starting to feel better was forgetting about them. I didn't want to forget, but I needed to move forward. Ultimately, I realized that they are always and will always be with me, and there will be a day when I can meet them, and tell them I love them while I hold them close.

I had a third work trip under my belt after coming back from Chicago and was starting to make some headway in terms of 2019 planning. The trip to Chicago was just what I needed at the time. I had the chance to make many new professional connections at Google and was really impressed by the team. It was the first Connecticut professional experience that felt "New York," in the way that I was able to connect with other professional people and have conversations where they were speaking my "marketing language," and it felt great. It felt motivating. I felt I had a strong plan for the year ahead and, after welcoming a new president to the team in January, was excited to share my vision with him. I remember having a one-to-one meeting with him, a "getting to know you" meet-and-greet type of meeting. I gave a summary of my experience, my vision for the company, and received rave reviews from him based on the feedback he had received from my superiors. Things seemed to be getting back to normal. Kevin and I agreed that we would try to get pregnant again after my birthday at the end of the month.

My birthday fell on a Monday. I remember because I had taken the day off. It was a new thing I was trying called taking care of myself. I had an appointment to get my hair colored and cut, a very special treat if you ask me after working in a hair salon for years. It is the same appreciation I have for good restaurant service and a great meal after being a cocktail waitress for years during my college days. Overall, I had a nice day filled with a dinner I didn't cook and quality time with my husband that evening. To say I was blindsided when my position was eliminated two days later would be an understatement.

It was just after 10:00 a.m. I had completed almost three hours of work for the day when human resources suddenly appeared. Now having HR in our office was not unusual. She typically liked to stop by every few days as a break from HQ where her office was, which was just a short drive from the distribution center where I worked, along with the marketing team and new president. I was escorted into the president's office, and it was all too familiar. This wasn't my first rodeo. My position was being eliminated. Translation: he was bringing in his former associate as CMO and didn't feel the director level was necessary. He shared that he had been in this position before, but he was sure "I'd land on my feet," blah, blah, blah. There were many things I wanted to say at that moment, but I had the wisdom to know that it didn't matter. There was nothing I could say to change his mind or my future; and so I wished him well, shook his hand, left his office, and went to pack up mine.

Looking back, I realize part of my disappointment wasn't about the job at all. Don't get me wrong, I was devastated to lose what I envisioned as a big opportunity. The job allowed me the chance to realize my goal of being a director of marketing. Remember those lists and goals I keep mentioning? It was saying good-bye to this new milestone, and what felt like a step ahead after taking so many steps back in my career. I realize now that it was also putting my personal goals on hold, my goal to start a family. It felt like a punch to the gut to literally lose my income just a few days after I felt ready to get pregnant again and had made the decision with Kevin to begin trying. It made me question if we shouldn't proceed. I mean, how could I in my right mind actively try to get pregnant when I didn't have a job and my future was uncertain?

I called Kevin immediately to tell him the news. I kept it together, but he knows me so well, I didn't have to voice that I was a mess inside. He insisted that he meet me at home regardless of how much I told him not to leave work. I cried the entire ride home and was happy to know that he would be meeting me there once I arrived. I was also happy I got there first and could compose myself so he wouldn't worry so much about me. There it is again, my desire to make others comfortable in my moments of despair. I had lost our first baby and my third job in six years. I went from having one employer in New York over the course of seven years to six jobs in six years. *Six jobs in six years.* Just wanted to emphasize that to make sure the comparison came through. To say that I felt like a failure would be a small inkling to the despair that I felt deep inside. Why did this keep happening to me? Why every time I felt like things were sorting themselves out would I be faced with another life-altering challenge? Just how strong did I have to be all the time? All questions I am still answering, although now I like to believe that I am closer to the answers. I also accept that the answers may change and I may never really know for sure.

Chapter 3

For the past few years, Kevin and I have spent Super Bowl weekend in Vermont with friends. What started out as a one-off trip has turned into a sort of tradition that is filled with lots of food (which clearly I love), me trying to ski (I've given up since those first three attempts), and relaxing fires in a real log cabin, as my friend Kelsey would say. We had the trip booked for months prior. It just so happened to land on the weekend after losing my third job. We were traveling with Kelsey and Andy, who were pregnant with their first, and Deann and Mike, who brought along their adorable one-and-a-half-year-old son George. While I was sincerely happy for Kelsey and Andy and enjoyed spending time with little George, it couldn't help but to shine a light on the fact that they both had something I yearned for, and still yearn for to this day. I am still grateful even now for how supportive everyone was and how much time they spent talking to us about my job loss and listening to my rambling thoughts of potential next steps. It felt like a healing weekend in that Kevin and I received the motivation needed to take a big step in a different direction. It also allowed me to grasp the feeling of a little more control over my destiny, something I so desperately needed.

Long before I met Kevin, he was actively mentoring special needs children in our community, in addition to his job as a special education teacher. He had forged a long-lasting relationship with his first mentee, Sabatino. It was this relationship, and the progress that he was able to make with Sabby, that motivated him to begin facilitating group programming for children and named these groups after Sabby—Social Sabby: teaching children with autism to be socially savvy. I, of course, learned of these social groups over the course of us dating and began helping him over the years by creating event flyers or volunteering during his day camps or autism-integration days he hosted.

Since I can remember talking to Kevin about his long-term goals, he always said his dream would be to make Social Sabby a real company and pursue it full time. This was a goal we shared. I remember wanting to be an entrepreneur since my early days in New York, thinking I would open my very own store one day. While both of our career paths took us in other directions, we both never lost the desire to be our own boss. In fact, my desire couldn't have been stronger after finding myself unemployed again for the third time. I found myself feeling directionless, in that I was so over being vulnerable. I was tired of being vulnerable in my career, my future always in the hands of someone that was unaware of my potential or frankly didn't care, months or years of work so easily tossed out the window on the whim of a decision from someone else. My efforts were starting to feel worthless, like it didn't matter what I brought to the table, how hard I worked, how much I put my job over my own needs. It really didn't matter. I saw jobs lost from my poor relationships with supervisors, or rather my incessant challenging of them, and jobs lost for no reason other than the desire for new management to bring in others they had established relationships with as a replacement for me. The only thing I could hold on to at that point was that me losing this last job was not a reflection of me or the job I did, but sometimes that even felt worse. It made me feel hopeless.

On the other hand, I felt vulnerable in my own skin in regards to what felt like a failure with my first pregnancy. Yes, I know it wasn't my fault, but it still wasn't the outcome I desired. I still wasn't able to get what I wanted. At the time when I finally felt like I was picking up the pieces of my shattered self, I was destroyed again professionally. I was left feeling stuck, like I couldn't move forward with getting pregnant because I was at a standstill in my career, again with no steady income after six months of the best salary I had ever realized. My plan had disappeared right before my eyes just as I was embarking on it.

It's ironic all those sayings that you know so well, and maybe even actually believe, but never really let sink in. The one that I am talking about for me is, "Everything happens for a reason." I had applied this thought to every single experience of my life thus far, but always in hindsight after the phoenix would rise from the ashes, never before. I could justify a job loss after a bigger and better opportunity was at my doorstep. This was the first time in my life where I felt I was able to be objective in the moment and apply this thought, this quote, in real time, with a little help from friends.

That Super Bowl weekend I spoke of my desire to be my own boss and open my own business. The main driver of this being the need for me to take control over my success for once. Are you starting to see a personality theme here? Yes, I needed some bit of control after feeling like I had lost the reigns of my own life. You never fully realize how much of your identity is tied to your job until you lose it. Now losing it three times, well, that's a real eye-opener. I mean, think about it. You're an adult, you meet someone new, and one of the first defining questions is, "What do you do?" When you can't answer that question, you're left wondering who you really are. Now granted, none of us are what we do, but isn't it interesting how closely they are tied? At least for me, I realized they were one in the same at that time. I think back to the pride I would feel telling my friends of my New York job and the experiences I had as a result. It had nothing to do with who I was (or am) as an individual. It was superficial, and it wasn't real.

It makes me question if we shouldn't be changing our perspective a bit about work and the relationship it has with your life. I think it would be wonderful to ask young children how they want to be remembered or what impact they would like to make in the world instead of, "What do you want to *be* when you grow up?" There is it right there. It is ingrained in us from adolescence: your job = who you will *be*. It's an odd thing for a super self-assured young woman that has experienced personal and professional success to receive hit after hit within a matter of a few years. I didn't realize I was carrying this weight all this time. I was in the middle of an identity crisis and now forced to face fertility issues at the same time. It was just too much to bear.

I knew I had to do something differently in order to get a different result. Quite frankly, I was so over (and still am) the idea of a traditional job. The thought of having a full-time position that I have to report into every day, take direction from someone else (I've learned that I never have really liked being told what to do), and work toward someone else's goal (big business) that wasn't doing something positive (i.e., selling something) couldn't have been further than what I wanted or needed. I started thinking outside of the box in terms of my experience and new skill sets acquired over the last few years. I spoke of marketing consulting and how I have always liked the idea of either taking on projects within a company or taking on independent clients. Consulting would give me the opportunity to have an income but never a permanent full-time position which seemed like a great avenue to explore.

On the other hand Kevin has been questioning his own career path and the longing desire to expand Social Sabby. The conversation quickly evolved to ways Kevin could provide services to families with special needs children and how I could use my marketing background to advertise the brand and build a website. It was odd that it seemed to make so much sense, but we had never talked about combining our efforts seriously before. It was so obvious now. Why not join forces, leverage his natural ability to work with special needs children and use my marketing experience to run the business behind the scenes?

The motivation provided by our friends that Super Bowl weekend in Vermont was what we needed to take it seriously. Sometimes you can question yourself on the viability of an idea (there's that word *viable* again), but to have it reinforced from others certainly gave an added boost of confidence. After what seemed like a really long conversation, we had decided to go for it. I would spend my time looking for a consulting gig and before getting hired would work to build a website and make Social Sabby a real business, by the state of Connecticut's requirements at least. We would also proceed with trying to get pregnant because we felt ready, and the reality was that I was now thirty-four and I wasn't getting any younger. *Tick-tock, tick-tock.*

If you haven't ever experienced divine intervention, it's understandable to be skeptical. If you've never experienced it, you might even not believe me when I tell you how effortlessly things started falling into place or all of the signs I began to see. (Yes, I believe in signs from the universe, or spirit guides, or guardian angels—all of the above, actually.) And if you've never been to a Reiki session, then you might even think I'm crazy (but please don't stop reading, there's some good gems left you don't want to miss). Super Bowl weekend 2019 came to a close, and Monday found us making the drive from snowy Vermont back to Connecticut.

Remember that haircut and color birthday treat to myself the week prior? My appointment was with a former student I met during my time at the cosmetology school I worked at. She had just opened up her new salon, and I wanted to congratulate her. I recall her sharing her goal with me while she was still in school, and I was so excited and proud that she had made it a reality. During my visit, we caught up on all of the things in our lives that had transpired since seeing her last. I didn't share my recent loss with her, and somehow the conversation got on the topic of Reiki. I shared it was something I was interested in and had learned a little about over the last year or so but had never experienced it firsthand. She provided a referral to me and recommended her so highly that I was thinking about making an appointment. Making an appointment was exactly what I did just before we left for Vermont. In hindsight, I think I was searching for answers and needed to look outside of myself. I was lucky to snag a spot the day after we returned from our weekend getaway.

It was Tuesday February 5, 2019, when I walked into the medical and wellness spa. I immediately felt at home. The space was warm, decorated like my home, and filled with lots of things I had grown to love over the last few years. I found crystals, sage bundles, and a deck of cards with an invitation to pick one while waiting. My card read, "I always trust the direction of the universe and know I'm being guided." Welp, felt like a pretty accurate message for me at the time. And yes, you naysayers, that could apply to lots of people…just wait. I got called in by a stunning woman who had an aura to match. You know when you meet someone and you get a vibe from them? It can be good or bad. Well, that is their energy, and I have learned to pay closer attention to this as I have gotten older. New people you meet or people you've known for a lifetime, I believe it is important to pay attention to how people make you feel. It is your subconscious reacting to their energy field and literally making you respond in a fight-or-flight fashion. This is my belief.

Her name is Miranda, and the hour appointment I had quickly turned into ninety minutes. She began by sharing that she believes in numerology, and since it was my first visit she wanted to start with my number. Turns out I was a number 7, and so this guided her selection of cards from her first deck. She selected seven cards and placed them in a clockwise circle, offering each one as a daily mantra that I would recite throughout the week and continue for a cycle of four weeks. The seven cards that I received were the following:

1. I am ready, thank you.
2. I am the weaver of my reality.
3. I forgive and let go with loving ease.
4. I am courageous, steady, and strong.
5. My emotions move through cycles and connect me to my truth.
6. I unleash my wildness and choose to be free.
7. My inner compass knows the way.

Each of these seven messages resonated with me for different reasons. I certainly felt ready to change my course completely and felt that I could create a new reality by taking charge of my career path. I was still working to forgive myself and others who I felt mistreated me in the recent past. I felt stronger for experiencing our loss and was feeling more courageous in starting a business. I felt that if I could be silent long enough with my own feelings, I could ultimately begin to make sense of them. I wanted to be free from the responsibility of someone else telling me what to do in a job and wanted to run wild with my own thoughts and desires without having to ask anyone else for permission first. Deep down I knew I would find my way and make it work. Ultimately, I felt like I had no other choice.

The next hour was spent with both a healing Reiki session but also a reading. The reading included Miranda describing my husband to a T, asking the significance of what "ten weeks" meant (messages she was receiving from spirit guides, my guardian angels during my visit) that I was the mother to an angel baby. That my pregnancy has served a purpose in deleting my fears of not being able to get pregnant, something I had never shared with anyone. She described physical symptoms I had and made recommendations to help. Although I did not have an ulcer, she told me I had ulcer-like symptoms and should drink celery juice, listen to the medical medium, and watch *The Secret* and *Heal* on Netflix—all things I did. She told me I was holding on to negative feelings so strongly in my core that it was actually manifesting in the physical symptoms I was experiencing (but that I had not shared with her).

She foreshadowed a consulting job I hadn't been approached about yet; made connections with colleagues at my last two employers that came true; and also made predictions for the last employer that I had just been released from, which recently closed its doors without any prior warning for two hundred plus employees. This was certainly impressive and, of course, emotional to have her acknowledge the loss of my first child. I spoke with her about my concerns to try to conceive again being unemployed, and she said she agreed with my husband in that I shouldn't wait and that everything would work out. Looking back, I now realize why she became so emotional speaking of us trying again, shedding tears in our session. In that moment I observed her to be very compassionate and emotionally available, made sense given her profession and abilities. Now I assume she must have seen our future losses and just felt sadness for what was to come.

There were two final cards that I picked from two more decks. One was an overview of my current state, the other was "homework" for me to research when I was home and should provide some type of direction or affirmation for the future. The first card I chose for the current state was, "My thoughts join a powerful swirling vortex of attraction." After watching *The Secret* on Netflix, this card resonated with me more. If you haven't seen this special, I would certainly recommend it. It is not for everyone, but is essentially focusing on the law of attraction. I couldn't help but feel that I was sabotaging myself with my endless hamster wheel of negative thoughts. I tried to give myself a break. I was still grieving, but I would make a conscious effort to utilize the mantra she provided to me for every occurrence in my day, whether it was negative or positive, which was to, "Thank it, bless it, let go with love and light." There was also this new perspective that there is no bad, only good. Everything is love, and everything is light. Similar to the idea of observing life and events outside of oneself to truly be objective, I find it amazing how much one's perspective can change when you are able to remove the eye of your own ego.

The second card I chose reflected the homework I was to do, after asking a question silently to myself three times. The card selected was the answer to the question I asked. The deck of cards was a combination of different Roman gods and goddesses, the idea being that the god or goddess you selected would represent your answer in some way. I selected the Roman goddess Vesta who represented "the home." In Greek mythology, Vesta is referred to as Hestia. They are one in the same. The question I asked myself before pulling this card was, "How do I know if now is the right time to start trying to conceive again?" The card read under Vesta's photo, "Your household situation is improving, either through a move or a healthy change in the occupants." A healthy change in my home's occupants? When I drew the card, even though Miranda had insisted the question be asked silently and kept to myself, she asked if I minded sharing it with her. When I did, she smiled and reminded me to read more about Vesta (Hestia) to find my answer.

Of course, the first thing I did when returning home was to begin Googling this goddess to see what she represented. I was shocked to discover her story and history. Let's see how well I can summarize this in my own words: Vesta is the goddess of the hearth and home, and it was her job to maintain what was described as a phallic flame. She had numerous Vestal Virgins whose job it was to keep the flame lit for one year until it was renewed during each

Roman New Year, on March 1. It is interesting that while she is a virgin, along with the Vestal Virgins, they were believed to hold power for procreation and symbolize the home and domesticity. In Roman mythology, fire is related to the conception of Roman heroes, and so it is easy to see the relation between Vesta, her phallic flame, and fertility. I recall reading that women would provide an offering to Vesta's hearth when trying to conceive.

So let me get this straight. I ask in my Reiki session, "How do I know if now is the right time to start trying to conceive again?" and the card I pull is a goddess associated with fertility? On top of that, the card pulled says my home will increase its occupants this year. It felt too aligned to be a coincidence, and I am starting to believe that there is no such thing as coincidences.

I decided I had spent enough of my first official day of unemployment not working, and so I decided to take the bull by the horns and start researching platforms for the website I was hell-bent on creating. For those of you that are not in the website space, once you select a platform, you want to use like WordPress or Squarespace, your next step is to select a theme for your website. A theme can be explained as a template for your website, it's basically the design, look, and feel of your site. Once selected, you then have the chance to add in your specific content (images, pages, product, etc.) and make it your own. It's probably an understatement to say that there are thousands of website themes to choose from. When I first began looking at WordPress, I noticed a library of over three thousand, and that is just one platform. I had an idea of the type of look I was going for, along with some newer scrolling features that I thought would make the website feel modern. Imagine my surprise when out of all the thousands of themes there are to choose from, the one that was first recommended to me was named Hestia.

Take it as you will; but this felt like a sign from the universe, divine intervention, someone was sending me a message. That I am sure of. I kind of sat at the table for a few minutes in disbelief. I even texted a girlfriend who I knew would understand because I needed to share it with someone in that very instant. Clearly, I felt like this was the theme I should be using, but first I had to check it out to see if it would meet our needs. Lo and behold, the newer scrolling feature I knew I wanted was included, along with every other requirement I had written down beforehand. What I thought was going to be the toughest decision for a person as indecisive as I am turned out to be the quickest one I had made in a while.

I got right to work, but it wasn't without its learning curves. While I had experience in prior roles with website re-platforms, creating content pages, and operating the backend of a website, I have never created one from scratch. It was such a liberating process to work from home and work on something that I could call my own. I realize now how empowering it was for me at that time to have something to show for the work I put into it. It was the complete opposite of my recent job experiences where I felt my work had been for nothing, the opposite of our efforts trying to conceive, in the end with nothing to show. I ended up spending many hours at my kitchen table the entire month of February, but at the end of the month I had something to show for my hard work, something tangible (sort of), something digital not physical. But it was real, and it was mine. The fact was that no one could take it away from me, and well, that was a good feeling. That is not to say I wasn't met with frequent bouts of hesitation, questioning if I was doing the right thing, but I continued forward nonetheless. It was as if I was being guided during this time by my own internal knowing. *My inner compass knows the way.*

I had been working on the website for about a week and a half when I received an e-mail from a recruiter that I hadn't worked with previously. She found me via my LinkedIn profile and was reaching out with a marketing consultant opportunity she thought I would be a good fit for. Approximately one and half weeks after I verbalized my desire to begin project-based consulting work and put that wish into the universe, I was contacted about a three-month project for a marketing consultant. Was the universe feeling bad about all of the negativity I had faced? Was I being thrown a bone? Did I manifest this opportunity, or was this positive karma for me? I didn't care. I felt happy, and I felt I was being directed to keep on this new path.

I interviewed for the job and was offered it pretty shortly afterwards. It was a three-month project, exactly the duration I had hoped for. I would work March to May and end just in time for when Kevin got out of school so we could work together over the summer on Social Sabby programs. I was in a good place with the website as I accepted this new project role and had a list (of course, there was a list) of the remaining tasks to be completed before I could launch the website for the world to see. Our goal was to have it up and running by the end of March, so we could advertise it at our upcoming Autism Integration Day that was to be held at our local high school where Kevin worked (and I was a graduate of) in April. One week before I reported to my new job, I learned I was pregnant for the second time.

My second pregnancy lasted five weeks and three days. I miscarried at home. It was a Monday. I recall experiencing this strange pain in my right side a few days before. It was alarming, but then again, anything is after surviving a miscarriage. I was trying to nurture more positive thoughts, for fear of not wanting to manifest another tragedy, and so when I felt that little twinge, I immediately worried and then immediately put the thought completely out of my head, or at least I tried to. I found myself thinking of that strange feeling a few times over the next few days but tried to not worry. I had a good sense of how far along I was since I had a previous cycle and, to be honest, was avoiding my doctor's office. Given my last visit, I was determined to wait longer. Knowing the immediate dos and don'ts of pregnancy, I felt I could wait for my first visit. I miscarried before I could even call to make an appointment.

My doctor's office ordered blood work to confirm what I already knew. Yes, I had been pregnant, and yes, my levels were dropping. When you miscarry at home, you don't need blood work to tell you what happened, but nonetheless, I went through the motions. It was four weeks into my new job, but I was still working a part-time schedule, and so I was grateful that I was home for when nature began to take its course. I picked myself up and kept going. I cried, but it was much less this time around. At the time, I felt I really took it in stride. There had been some positive messages I felt I had received, and quite frankly, I couldn't fathom the idea that something was wrong, and so I buried my grief. April came and went, and I noticed myself beginning to decline. I had one more month of my consulting project to get through, I had launched the website, and Kevin and I hosted our largest Social Sabby Autism Integration Day ever during April's Autism Awareness Month. In looking back, I think I was so numb from our two losses that I again buried myself in work and focused on everything external so I wouldn't have to acknowledge or address my innermost feelings.

To say that May was a disaster is an understatement. I had the mindfulness during that time to believe that my wave of depression was being onset by what would have been our approaching due date of our first child. I remember being so excited to be due in May, perfect to enjoy a summer off with my new babe, with my husband who would also be off. Too good to be true it certainly was. I felt like I was back to square one, only this time it was worse. Now I was faced with coming to terms with the loss of two children and no closer to any type of understanding as to why this was happening. My daydreams of what the ease of death could bring pushed me to make an appointment with my doctor. I knew it was okay to be grieving, but the sadness that enveloped my every thought and interaction became too much to bear. It started to feel like something was wrong, and somehow I found the courage to reach out.

I remember sitting in the doctor's office, and as I began describing how I was feeling, I was overcome with emotion and couldn't hold back my tears. She is a wonderful doctor who has a wonderful bedside manner, and so she was very gracious at that moment. I somehow felt weak as I shared my uncontrollable emotions. I couldn't hold it together. I couldn't be strong. I couldn't put on a brave face, I just couldn't. I asked her why after months I was feeling worse. Her hypothesis was that I hadn't fully grieved our first loss, and now we were faced with a second, that maybe I hadn't been ready to try again and that it was okay to give ourselves more time. Based on the variety of symptoms I was experiencing and thoughts I was having, she diagnosed me with having postpartum depression.

I was angry at first, maybe even confused. I looked at her and said, "I thought that was only a possibility after delivering a baby." To which she corrected me in that it is defined as depression as a result of hormonal changes that occur from pregnancy. Great, so now, not only have I lost two babies, but I am suffering from postpartum depression. She encouraged me to seek out resources she referred me to—a list of therapists, potential prescriptions, etc.—but none of them felt right. I couldn't even talk to close friends about what happened, how can I talk to a stranger? A pill to make me feel better? It wasn't on my list of potential remedies. I guess I just felt like I was supposed to be sad, I was supposed to be angry. I lost two children. There wasn't a pill that could bring them back. I felt that the only way out of these feelings was through them, and even if a pill could bring me some relief in the short-term, it almost felt inauthentic. I didn't want to trick my brain into thinking I was happy when clearly I wasn't. I hope these statements do not offend anyone that is finding help through a prescription. I support each person finding their own way. It's just that for me, this wasn't it.

The one suggestion I was happy to hear was that we could begin fertility testing if I so desired. She did mention that many times testing wouldn't begin until experiencing a third loss, but that given my age we could start sooner. I jumped at the chance to get some real answers. The only testing we had undergone to date was an evaluation of our baby that was removed via my D&C last September. It was optional testing to see if there were any genetic issues we should be aware of, but thankfully everything came back normal. I left her office with a multitude of blood work orders, a referral for a fertility office, and a urologist for Kevin. To both our relief and dismay, every single test we had came back with typical levels. There was no smoking gun we could tie to our losses, and it was extremely unsettling. We can put a man on the moon, but no one can tell me why I am losing my babies? It seemed so unfair and also like a slap in the face. With so much technology and medical advancement, I felt I (along with every other woman) deserves more, deserved better, deserves this to be a priority. I deserved an answer.

I proceeded with scheduling an appointment with the fertility office, even though I wasn't sure it was the right step. Be it my ignorance at the time or maybe the feeling that I didn't want there to be something wrong, I felt like *fertility* was the wrong word to describe our situation because I was able to get pregnant. It was staying pregnant that was the real challenge for me. I think I was just lashing out internally and also aggravated that we had to wait three months for an appointment. Didn't they know it had already been almost a year since we first began trying? It was both frustrating to have to wait, but also in some way made me feel confident in the office that they were booked so far in advance. It had to be for a good reason, I assured myself.

I tried my best to get back to my normal self, but there were still some really dark days ahead. I received an invitation from a girlfriend to join her in Vegas for a long weekend along with some of our mutual friends. I remember thinking I couldn't go because it would be my last week of my consulting job. I was also still severely depressed and not doing anything really to help myself. I turned to substances to ease my pain and began drinking more frequently. I realize this is quite the contradiction to everything I just said about taking a pill. For some reason having a glass (or three) of wine seemed more harmless. I didn't need a prescription, just a quick drive to my local package store (as we call them in Connecticut). That's liquor store for everyone else. I continued this for several weeks.

While I knew deep down that Vegas was the furthest thing from what I needed, I also needed a distraction. And maybe a change of scenery would do me good? It didn't help my decision that Kevin was going on a guy's trip to New Orleans that same weekend. A week beforehand I changed my mind and booked a ticket. I spent the next five days in sin city drowning my sorrows and indulging in food, fun, and anything else that would keep my mind occupied. It wasn't long before I found myself at a bar with one of my girlfriends spilling the beans about my two losses. There I was, at a bar in Vegas at 1:00 p.m., crying my eyes out. It felt good to share, but at the same time I didn't want to think about it. I mean, clearly, I had flown across the country running from my feelings and an empty house that I don't think I could bear without Kevin. I flew home a few days later, greeted by him. I was happy to be home and to see him, but not much else.

It was back to work right away. Now was the time we had been waiting for, a summer off to work together on Social Sabby. We had a jam-packed schedule, with more events in a calendar year offered than ever before. We started to see the fruits of our labor with new member referrals, great feedback from participants and parents, and what seemed like a growing network online. We hosted life skills workshops in June with cooking, technology, and social recreational focuses, followed by a one-week long summer camp and also a "Ballin 4 Autism" basketball tournament with our local YMCA. We had given ourselves the month of July off, and Kevin's brother was getting married at the end of the month, and so we had many happy occasions to look forward to with family. I don't know if it was the positive energy we both felt from our accomplishments in June; the fact that we were getting to spend more time together, which felt healing in itself; or maybe it was the pressure from the ticking clock, but we decided to try again. And I got pregnant immediately.

We enjoyed the month of July. Our second wedding anniversary passed, and we were feeling pretty good. I tried so hard to be present in the moment, and looking back, I think I did a pretty good job recognizing and being grateful for our successes along with way, given the overall circumstances and the fact that I was nervous about my third pregnancy. We welcomed a sister into our family, someone I am so grateful that Brian chose. Alexis has been such a joy to get to know and has shown me so much kindness over the course of our losses. The week after their wedding, we crossed paths in Newport. They had taken an extra-long weekend after the wedding to get away before their honeymoon next winter, and Kevin and I had randomly planned to go for a few nights before our last week of summer camp that was scheduled in August. There was one day of overlap between our trips, and so we met for lunch before going our separate ways.

It was at the lunch that we shared we were expecting for the third time. I think Brian already knew from Kevin, but pretty sure it was news to Alexis. I, unfortunately, was not able to keep it a secret from some family members at their wedding the weekend prior. I think it was a combination of my lack of adult beverage in hand and Kevin spilling the beans, something I was not too happy about if I am being honest. I was actually very annoyed at first, given our history but also was trying to go with the flow and take things as they come. Once I overcame my initial anger, I let it go and enjoyed telling a few people myself. I guess at that moment I felt that I shouldn't be afraid to share our news, even though it was early on, I wanted to allow myself to feel joy about the pregnancy and not fear.

That Saturday we were off to our friend's son George's second birthday party. I was looking forward to celebrating him and also seeing Lena, it was her first public outing since Kelsey and Andy welcomed her in June. I was also cautiously optimistic about my own little bundle of joy that we were expecting to welcome March 2020. I ended up speaking with one of the party guests that I had met several times over the years. As we made small talk, her son ran by and she tried to convince him to sit and eat something, a difficult task for a third grader at a birthday party filled with fun and friends. We both kind of chuckled as he ran off, unwilling to sit for a moment to eat. I innocently asked if that was her only son, and I never could have imagined the story that question would bring up or me speaking with her for almost the entire length of the party, which was several hours.

She went on to share that he was her miracle baby. She had suffered from seven miscarriages in addition to a stillbirth well into her third trimester. My heart broke for her as she shared her experience of loss. It made me feel that my losses were insignificant in a way. This poor woman went through such heartache. I cannot imagine being so far along and then not only having to experience the grief of losing your child, but then having to endure the experience of labor knowing your child isn't coming home with you. I found myself being grateful for miscarrying earlier in my pregnancy. Now, of course, I know my losses are still significant; but I couldn't help but to feel compassion for her painful path to parenthood.

There were two large takeaways I had from this exchange. The first being that I don't think the sadness you experience as a parent in this situation every truly goes away. I equate it to any other loss you experience. You grow to accept that you have lost a person, but the pain never fully goes away. It changes and evolves. As I stood there and watched her wipe fresh tears for losses from years prior while she watched her healthy third grader play, I knew that I was in fact facing a new normal. I had to accept that I would forever be impacted by our losses and that wouldn't change even if we were lucky enough to experience the arrival of a healthy child earthside one day.

The second and more terrifying realization that I still face today is that I will not feel safe in any future pregnancy until well after the baby has arrived. I always felt that the three-month rule was your safe bet. It was safe to announce your pregnancy after twelve weeks because most miscarriages happen before that time. It was certainly the case with my first two losses. I went home with this nagging fear that I wouldn't be able to enjoy my pregnancy at all. I would be battling fears of losing them until I held them in my arms, and maybe even longer. I was now worried about SIDS and establishing a new "safe barometer" for when I could enjoy the blessing that is a child.

I was seven weeks and two days pregnant. It was Saturday, August 3, the same day as George's second birthday party. I had received a positive test from my doctor in July and had convinced the fertility office to keep our appointment for August 19, despite their suggestion to cancel when I called to share our pregnancy. I remember the phone call a few weeks earlier with their office and them stating that there was no need to keep the appointment since I was pregnant. After offering congratulations, they shared that the purpose of their office was to get patients pregnant before sending them back to their ob-gyn. Since I was already pregnant, I didn't need the appointment. I expressed concern on canceling given the three months it took to get the appointment, in addition to our history, and not wanting to cancel since it was still a few weeks away. They obliged my request and said if I was still pregnant a few days before the appointment to call and cancel.

I began to miscarry Sunday, August 4. It was the day before our last Social Sabby summer camp. To say that this miscarriage was unlike the others is a severe understatement. In the past I experienced emotional and spiritual suffering. This time those sentiments were accompanied by uncompromising physical pain. My body was surely recognizing this miscarriage, and I remember wondering if the pain I felt was what labor was like. In fact, my body was going through the physical changes to release the baby from my body. The body aches, harsh stomach cramping, and feelings of hopelessness were too much to bear. All of this a day before our largest ever Social Sabby summer camp was set to begin. We had over twenty-five children signed up, and the thought of having to work the camp was something I could not even imagine. Physically, I was keeled over in pain for three days. I stayed in bed and only left when absolutely necessary or to shower. Meanwhile, I left my grieving husband to tackle our joint responsibility alone. He, of course, was strong for the both of us as he had been the last two times; but he was grieving too and I couldn't be there for him because I was literally beside myself. I remember avoiding calls from everyone that knew. I know they meant well in reaching out, but I didn't want to speak to anyone. I was inconsolable, and there were no words anyone could say.

I remember feeling so guilty for leaving Kevin for the first two days of camp, but honestly, I had no other choice. By the fourth day he started to suggest that I try to go for a half day as a distraction. I know he meant well and wanted to see me get out of bed, but at the time I felt slightly resentful that he was trying to push me to pick myself up. I simply wasn't ready. Despite my inner feelings of not wanting to leave the house, let alone have to speak to people and hide this very real life-changing event, I opted to go to the camp for the final three days since some of my physical symptoms had started to improve.

In any other circumstance, work may have been a welcome distraction. Working with children however was the furthest from that. Here I was, still not only physically and emotionally dealing with a miscarriage in real time, I was surrounded with children. Even my best efforts to focus on the tasks at hand were met with thoughts of me never being able to have children of my own. I was able to trick myself into thinking our first loss was a fluke and that the second was an anomaly, but a third was inconceivable, unexplainable. There had to be a reason, and I was determined to figure out what it was. Kevin saw how much I was struggling and suggested I take breaks whenever needed. I found myself alone wandering the halls of my old high school crying, praying that I would not see another soul in that moment, let alone someone I knew.

Looking back, I am not exactly sure how I managed to get through the week but I did. I braved each new day by suppressing my own personal feelings and trying to focus on the positive impact we were having in these children's lives. In a way, I started to view them as my kids, and as sad a thought as it was, I started to accept that these may be the only kids Kevin and I get to have a hand in raising. Not that we are raising kids with Social Sabby in anyway, that would be an overstatement, but I mean that these might be the only kids that Kevin and I get to share in childhood experiences with. I was both grateful for that and hurt at the thought at the same time.

Chapter 4

August was a blur. Just as I thought I had experienced the depths of my despair, I reached rock bottom. I was numb and had lost any desire to try to move forward. Everything felt so pointless and meaningless. I felt like I would never experience happiness again. I had told myself that "third time's the charm." But to lose our third child was unbearable, mind-boggling. What did I do to deserve such heartbreak? I finally verbalized my feelings with Kevin, the feelings I had suppressed, the thoughts I was avoiding but kept surfacing.

I will never forget how Kevin reacted when I told him I didn't want to live anymore. You can imagine how hard that would be to hear from the person you love, the person you are building a life with. To have the person you promised to spend your life with tell you they don't want to live it anymore must have been devastating for him. He was obviously so concerned and immediately said that we needed to get someone else involved. If I remember correctly, I think he wanted me to go to the hospital. I refused because I knew that I was not an actual danger to myself, and I knew enough about hospital protocol that I was in fear of being committed in a psychiatric ward. I knew the consequences of voicing my feelings publicly, and it was not appropriate for my situation, but then again, I didn't know what was. I knew though that the feelings of depression had become too much for me to manage on my own. To this day I am glad that I communicated my deepest and darkest thoughts, but I still feel guilty for feeling them and sharing them with him and making him worry about me in a way I never thought possible. I realize now that it was a necessary evil because without his help I would have not reached out for help. To this very day, now January 2020, as I sit at my desk with tears streaming down my face recalling this day, I am filled with sadness that I somehow disappointed him by falling apart. Even though he never communicated this to me or showed any inkling that was what he was feeling, I projected my own feelings of inadequacies on him. I felt I wasn't the wife I was supposed to be to him, that I was no longer the person he had married. How unfair to him that he not only had to suffer our losses but now had to be worried about my mental health when I am sure he was wrestling with his own as well.

Reflecting back on this time in the present moment, I am filled with conflicting emotions. I feel selfish, vulnerable, even childlike. I felt a type of restlessness I hope that you cannot and will not ever understand. I felt anger again, followed by hopelessness, again. I was deep in a cycle of depression without a desire to get out. It started to feel that I would have to find a way to live day to day with the most intense feelings of despair. This had been my reality for so long, I forgot what it was like to live a normal happy day or not feel lonely even when in a crowded room filled with family and friends. It seemed that this was my new normal. It felt like life was just going by as it normally did for everyone else, and I was an outsider looking in on myself playing the role of who I used to be.

I have learned things about myself through the course of these life experiences. I have learned that one of the hardest things for me to do is ask for help or show vulnerability. It's like I have this sick and demented character trait that handling things independently makes me strong. I couldn't have been any further from the truth. I started to feel that maybe talking to a stranger would be easier than someone I knew. I started to feel that if I wasn't able to release all of the horrible thoughts and feelings I was having, they would eventually swallow me whole or, worse, manifest in my body in the form of some life-threatening illness or disease. Sometimes it felt like my thoughts were making me physically ill, but there was nothing I could do to change it. It was this devastating cycle of sadness, despair, anger and guilt, with each emotion leading into one another with no end in sight.

As we awaited our upcoming appointment with the fertility clinic, I tried to focus on the gratitude I felt for being able to keep the appointment despite our positive pregnancy test. I was grateful to have the insight to keep it. I was also devastated and angry that I was right in thinking we might still need it. It almost made me feel guilty in a way that I had a backup plan, that I didn't truly believe this pregnancy would be any different than our first two. It is a realization that is compounded every time I think of a future pregnancy. The reality is that I will never have the luxury of enjoying a pregnancy. I will forever be scarred by these experiences. This was a part of death I was still learning to navigate, not only are you grieving your loss but also grieving all of the life events that should bring happiness. Instead of thinking of the courage required of me to continue trying to conceive, I thought it best to focus on one day at a time, sometimes taking each day hour by hour. It was during this time that I found the list of therapist referrals my ob-gyn had given me back in May that I had tucked away for this type of day when the rain was just too heavy.

As I began researching the list of therapists, I thought it best to first see which were in network with my insurance provider. A sad but real concern to have during this time is the expense piece of the process. I was determined to not have the experience of unexpected bills arise having learned this lesson just a year prior. We opted for genetic testing with my D&C procedure, an elective test that ended up costing us thousands of dollars out of pocket. Nothing like adding financial stress to an already dire situation to make you want to keep pushing your head through a wall.

I slowly began winding down the list of potential options so that I could spend more time determining who, if anyone, could be the right fit for me. All along during this process, I was still unsure if I would actually pursue scheduling a meeting. I was unsure if this was the right thing for me, but for the time being, it felt like a small step forward, something was telling me this was what I should do, and so I proceeded. *My inner compass knows the way.*

After I was able to identify a short list of therapists to research further, I began reading the doctor profiles available on my insurance website. It was disheartening reading about each person and not feeling like any were the right fit or someone I would feel comfortable speaking to. That was until I found the online profile of Paige McMullen. She had a private practice in Middletown, which was a short fifteen-minute ride from my home. In reading her short bio, it was the first time I felt that her therapy areas of focus really resonated with me. She spoke of anxiety, self-identity, and role changes associated with relationships and motherhood. What solidified my desire to reach out was her mention of work with postpartum depression and a focus on the period of women's reproductive lives, maternal behavioral, and mental health. Finally, I thought, a woman whom I could feel comfortable speaking with, that specialized in my areas of concern, was in network, and only fifteen minutes away. It seemed too good to be true.

I somehow mustered up the courage to pick up the phone and call. I must admit this took me longer than I had hoped, but I was glad I was finally taking the first step toward addressing my mental health with a professional. I called her directly and was met with her voice mail message. As I listened to her greeting, my heart sank as she stated on the message that she was not currently accepting any new patients. It was almost as if her message hit me physically. The one small twinge of hope I'd felt in a long time was gone in an instant. It felt it was too good to be true that I had found her, so of course, it wouldn't work out. Of course, she wasn't accepting new patients. Why would I expect anything different, given the string of bad luck we had experienced with our first three pregnancies? This certainly was aligned with our recent course of life events, but I was extremely disappointed nonetheless. It felt like as soon as I had gathered the courage to reach out, something that was especially difficult for me to do, to even acknowledge that I couldn't do it alone, I was turned down without even having the chance to speak with her.

I hung up the phone and went back to my list, only to spend the next hour or so confirming that there was no one else I wanted to even attempt to reach out to. I didn't feel like they were someone I could confide in with my innermost feelings, and if that's not possible, I thought, *What is the point of even trying?* I decided to call

Paige again. I would leave a message and take a chance. I certainly had nothing to lose. I called her again later that afternoon and left a message when she did not answer. I shared on my voice mail that I had experienced three losses over the last twelve months and that I understood that she was not accepting new patients but that in reading her online bio she was the only therapist that resonated with me and I asked if she had a waiting list I could be added to. I shared that I would be willing to wait to meet with her because something told me that she was the person I should be speaking with. She returned my call the following day and said that the message I left her moved her and she was willing to meet with me but that her availability may be limited. I was thrilled. I felt a new sense of hope and gratitude for pushing myself to call her back and leave that message. It was the best decision I had made for myself up until this point.

I met with Paige for the first time on August 20, 2019. It was a Tuesday. This meeting came just one week after Kevin and my initial fertility consultation at UConn and just over two weeks since our third loss. The initial meeting was awkward for me, and I shared this with her. I told her that I had never met with a therapist before and that it felt out of character for me, also that I was a person who struggled to ask for help and so the idea of reaching out to a stranger was almost uncomfortable in a way. She said that she understood and that it was a typical feeling expressed by first-time patients. She asked what brought me to see her, or rather to elaborate on the message summary I had left, and what drove me to reach out. I told her that despite my hesitation, I finally got to the point where my thoughts scared me. I shared that I felt like I needed a professional to speak with because although Kevin had been supportive and listened to me, I didn't think it was fair to him to always be my sounding board. I wanted to speak with someone who was well versed in the subject of postpartum depression, someone that could help to give me the tools I needed to cope with my depression. That hopefully, through verbalizing some of my heaviest, darkest fears and thoughts, I would start to feel a bit lighter.

The hour session was gone in an instant. Our first meeting went okay enough that I decided to go back again the following week. In the meantime, she gave me a small packet of questions to complete and bring with me to the following session. The one question that stuck out to me, and that I can recall today, asked what goals I wanted to achieve through therapy. I remember sharing that I was hoping to obtain tools that could help me work through my depression and negative thought patterns, that I wanted to vocalize my recurring thoughts in hopes that releasing them would make them less likely to reappear, but that, most of all, I wanted to get back to my normal self. I wanted my perspective to change, to be more positive and not meet each day with doom and gloom, a struggle that rises still today but now less frequently.

Our second meeting continued on as the first had. This time I was a bit more comfortable sharing more of my story. Before the session ended, we spent some time reviewing the packet she had given me the week prior and my written answers. It was at this time that she questioned what I meant by my desire to return to my "normal self." This sparked a conversation that I now think of daily. She opened my eyes to the fact that not only do our experiences make us who we are, they also shape our perspectives. The fact was that I had to embrace that I was fighting every day, that our losses have forever changed the person that I was. These events have changed my perspective, and so it has also changed my reality, my life. Maybe my desire to return to my old self was really my desire to be the person I was before all the despair and lost hope. I wanted to desperately be the wide-eyed optimistic person I had always been, but that person was gone forever.

My focus had to be working through these depressive thoughts and feelings and also accept that they were valid and needed attention and care. The old me never put myself first. This is one lesson I am grateful for. I needed to stop being so judgmental and critical of myself. A large part of this was related to my concern of how others perceived me. I felt many times, as most people do, concerned about how my actions, or lack thereof, would appear to others. It was a strange realization that after thinking I was so independent and living my life for myself, to know that I had been making decisions out of fear and not always for myself. Fear of negative consequences, fear of not "doing the right thing," fear of how my choices would make others feel despite how they made me feel—I was done with all of it. I was now only making decisions out of love. I was done compromising myself for others. I felt that if I was always authentic with my true self from that moment on, and what I believed to be right for me, that I could not go wrong. I felt like things or people that shouldn't be in my life would naturally start to fall away, and I am grateful that I was right.

Throughout the course of my therapy, which has only been a few months, I have felt more empowered and more self-assured. I have been able to identify negative patterns in my life that have been in existence long before our first loss. I was able to finally see how much I compromised myself for others or the greater good of my life scenarios. I have realized how much I internalize and many times obsess over my feelings or events that have transpired with others. I see how this pattern that was developed over the course of my life now played out with my postpartum depression. I replayed the series of events over and over again in my mind the way I had with other disappointments or disagreements in my life. Torturing myself over negative events in my life wasn't new, but my awareness of it certainly was.

When I first reached out to begin therapy, I was focused on my depression and despair. I wanted to find a "quicker" fix to my feelings. I needed outside help after feeling so low for a year but what felt like a lifetime. I just needed help and someone to listen without judgment, but also give me unbiased feedback. What I found, and already knew, is that there is no fix. Just as our experiences shape our perspectives, we have the power to change our thoughts and therefore our reality. This is *much* harder to do than to say, but I started small and still use this today. One tactic I applied was every time I found myself thinking a negative thought, I would actively replace it with something I was grateful for. The things I thought of were as basic as a hot shower, a place to rest my head, a hot meal. This helped to give me perspective on all of my blessings. Many times I found myself being grateful for Kevin. He is the only person that truly knows this experience with me, and I was grateful to have him with me through it all.

Although this was a valid start to try to change my negative perspective, I was still grieving and still yearned for someone else's story that made me feel heard, made me feel understood. Paige had provided a few books to me to see if any resonated with me. Of the five to six books she provided, none gave me the feelings I was seeking out. While many of them had glimmers of emotions that mirrored mine, there was nothing that really spoke to me. Time I had set aside for more self-care, including reading these inspirational books, somehow made me feel more isolated. As I read hopeful story after hopeful story, I somehow felt guilty for still feeling such despair. Despite our third loss being so fresh, it had been a year since our first and six months since our second. It felt like I was never able to fully get a grip because just as I was working through my feelings and gathering the courage to move forward, we were hit with another loss. Many of the books I read had sad endings. One women lost her marriage from the stress their losses put on her relationship with her husband; another marriage failed based on her husband's desire for a family, which he sought out in a new marriage; and many others did not conceive, either by choice or because they physically were not able to.

Where were the happy endings that are ingrained in us from childhood? On one hand I wanted to feel heard from others that had a similar experience of loss. I wanted to feel validated for such aggressive and negative thoughts, but I also wanted to be lied to. I wanted someone to tell me that it was going to be okay, even though I knew it might not be. I wanted to be told that I would have a healthy and happy baby of my own in my arms one day, but no one could tell me that either, and even if they did, I wouldn't have believed them anyway. The sad truth of the matter is that I didn't even know what I wanted or needed. It changed daily, even sometimes moment to moment, and that in itself was so frustrating. How could I help myself if I didn't even know which step was the right one to take or what type of support I needed? I felt like a minefield. One wrong statement or thought made and I would be blown to a million pieces. It was absolute despair.

It sometimes felt that all my energy had to be spared for my now biweekly therapy appointments. Before suffering from depression, I never realized how much energy was required to shower and get dressed for the day, with the knowledge that you would be faced to see or engage with other people. Many times, this was the only time I left the house for several weeks. I was now accustomed to having daily needs like groceries and such delivered, and I avoided human interaction for some time. I was, and still am, unemployed; and so I was grateful to not have the responsibility of being at a workplace by a certain time each day and be faced with actual conversations. I was, and am, much happier home alone. I never realized how much time and space is required to really work through one's own thoughts. I simply did not have the mental capacity to speak to others other than my husband, and so many calls and texts went unanswered, and that was okay.

When I physically felt like I could return to yoga, I did. The mental benefits I realize from yoga are undeniable, and so I am grateful to have had my practice to lean on during that time in my life. Even more so than the physical practice, I found the meditation to be so healing. Even though it was short-lived, in those few moments of silence on my mat, I felt a small sense of peace. It's not that thoughts of our losses or my sadness didn't present themselves. Of course, they did. But instead of meeting those thoughts with anger or more sadness, I simply accepted them. It's almost as if I was trying to observe my thoughts outside of my own ego and emotion, and even though the moments were fleeting, they felt good enough to keep me coming back for more.

A few more weeks passed, and I was now feeling well enough to prioritize a few outings weekly. Every week I attempted to make it to two yoga classes, in addition to my husband's Friday-night football games. Over the years I had made friends with some of the other coaches' wives, one in particular. Linda and I always sat together. She was aware of our losses, and it was comforting to be around someone who knew what was going on in our lives but was also respectful enough to let me talk about it when I wanted to and didn't bring it up when I didn't. I was also met by two childhood friends this past season—Natasha, whose son was playing on the team, and Denise, whose eighth-grade daughter was now the age where she was interested in attending high school football games. I was grateful to have them there. It was nice to be able to see them on a weekly basis, and it became a new routine that I actually really looked forward to. We even joked that it was like we were in high school again going to the Friday-night games. Thinking of it now, I think it did feel like the "old times" I was so desperately craving, when life was so much simpler and less complicated. It was a welcomed weekly date for sure.

That's just how it happens. You don't change one day to be happy or your normal self again, but there will be little windows, sometimes only tiny cracks, that remind you that you can find joy again, you can find things to look forward to again, you can find reasons to want to live again. Something as small as a yoga class, a few hours in the bleacher stands with good friends and good conversation, cheering on your husband's team to win, or a scheduled meeting with your new therapist can lift you up enough to want to keep going. The one thing that they all have in common is that they are all distractions from the one thing I was allowing to rule my brain and my life. I was so focused on the one thing that wasn't working out for me that I was failing to see all the beauty and blessings that were in my life.

I find it interesting how our minds can work sometimes and how differently people can respond to similar situations. For me I always viewed myself as overall happy and optimistic; but what the last year and a half has shown me is that I am also very critical, judgmental, and extremely hard on myself. I am so goal oriented that I don't allow myself the opportunity to enjoy the journey because I am so focused on the destination. When I look back on my life so far, I wonder if I had been missing the point all along. My new perspective tells me that the beauty of life is in the journey and the lessons we learn along the way.

As my husband and I embarked on the path to parenthood, we never could have imagined the roads before us. We viewed our baby as the destination, not knowing how many detours of life lessons would be waiting for us along the way. I still wonder if our losses are our first lessons in parenthood. That if we are lucky enough to have a child earth side one day, we must accept that nothing is really within our control and that the experience is both beautiful and heartbreaking at the same time. That every day your child gets older is simply a day closer to them living their own lives and the day you mourn the little child whose every need depended on you. It makes me think of the cycle of life, the same way the changing colors of the fall leaves once did. Now as I gaze outside of my window on this cold winter day, the trees are bare and there are remnants of snow from the last storm a few weeks ago. In just a few short months the temperature will start to warm, and spring will be around the corner. The seasons are a reminder that the only constant is change and that even when time feels like its standing still, it is in fact still moving forward. And so I continued pushing as well, in hopes to move forward.

Chapter 5

I was impressed by our appointment at CARS, the Center for Advanced Reproductive Services. It was lengthy, but the time spent was very thorough, and we left feeling more informed. I was most touched by the structure of our appointment. It felt that the office truly understood our perspective and allowed us the time for all our concerns to be addressed, with a variety of different individuals. We met with Dr. Grow, his nurse, and others to review our history. I had a full internal exam, and then met with the doctor in his office to review the results of his findings from the internal ultrasound. He stated that I had a septate uterus, and while it was a minor case, it can severely increase the risk for miscarriage. A septate uterus is a condition that women are born with, and in layman's terms, instead of the top of my uterus being a straight line across, it had a small widow's peak that would penetrate the womb. Although my measurements were a mere 33mm, further independent research showed an 80 percent miscarriage rate as a result of my condition, in contrast to the typical 10–20 percent miscarriage rate. Based on the plethora of blood work and testing I had undergone, and the fact that all of my results were typical to date, made Dr. Grow that much more confident that we had found a smoking gun.

He discussed corrective options with us, which were all various forms of procedures I could undergo. He made his recommendation and then escorted us to the financial advisor that would review all costs with us and confirm what our responsibility would be, if any, after reviewing with our insurance carrier. Clearly this office knew what they were doing. Within a single appointment, they identified something in me that needed correcting, took time with us to answer any and all questions, made recommendations, and then had isolated time for financial and insurance review. I certainly felt like I was in good hands, and so the next agenda item on the list was to schedule the surgery as soon as possible.

I remember this time being so stressful, we had met our $4,000 insurance deductible, but our plan was set to expire at the end of August. The UConn office was aware of this and was diligently working to get the surgery scheduled before the end of the month so that we would not have any expense out of pocket. The large caveat here is that I had not yet had a cycle after our last loss earlier in the month. Apparently, there is specific timing for when the procedure can be performed, and it has to be within certain days of your cycle for safety precautions and the highest success rate. Although a date was available, I couldn't be scheduled until I got my period. I never wanted my cycle to come so badly, but of course, it didn't happen in August.

I remember calling the office in September to alert them that my cycle had come, and them sharing with me the potential need for me to begin birth control pills to control my cycle for ease of scheduling the surgery. They assured me that I could stop taking them as soon as the procedure was completed, but this didn't sit well with me for several reasons. I had just experienced my third loss, and my hormones were all over the place, as they had been for the last year. I had made the decision over a year ago to stop taking birth control, partly because we wanted to begin trying to get pregnant, but another reason I was especially happy to stop taking the pill is because I had so many issues with birth control over the years.

I remember a time in college when I thought I was having a panic attack. I was a sophomore in my dorm and remember being inconsolable. It was odd, it was as if I could only think of negative things in my life or things that I felt warranted a complaint. It was the first time that I didn't feel in control of my own emotions. I remember calling my mother trying to explain and then realizing it was a mistake for me to be speaking with anyone, I was out of control. The strange thing is that these feelings of despair were then met with the total opposite emotion, extreme happiness the following day. I started to think that maybe I was bipolar, and so I made doctors' appointments with my primary physician and also my ob-gyn.

I was not bipolar, but my ob-gyn suggested that we try a different type of birth control that had a lower hormone rate. To say that this made all the difference was an understatement. I was glad that I had begun charting these "episodes" and was able to track them closely to my cycle. It was literally like clockwork, once a month I would feel like the world was ending, only to feel fine the very next day. The newer prescription helped for some time, but I found myself switching several times before finding one that I was able to stay on. The feeling never sat well with me that this medication was impacting my hormonal balance, but I incorrectly thought it was a necessary evil in my life, knowing I was not ready to start a family.

In that one conversation with the nurse from UConn, all of those college memories and doctors' appointments and feelings of despair and anger arose. I thought, *My body has been through enough, and I do not want to add more hormones to the mix.* I shared my concerns on taking the pill, and the reaction received was one of surprise. I am sure that in their professional experience working in a fertility office, they are met with individuals willing to do anything to conceive, but I was not willing to compromise myself or what I felt was right for my body. They said they would try their best to get me scheduled within the small window of time, and luckily for me, they were able to make it work and get me scheduled the following week.

In the meantime, Kevin had made an appointment with a urologist to undergo additional testing. We wanted to rule out all potential concerns and so he underwent blood work and multiple rounds of semen analysis. His second round of testing happened to fall on the same day as my procedure, and so my mother took me to the surgery. I remember being disappointed that Kevin wasn't there. I had told him that it was okay, but this was an example of me not communicating what it was that I really needed. I am certainly better about this now.

I recall waking up and my mother being in the room shortly after. Whether it was the anesthesia or months of pent-up emotions,

I could no longer hold it in and so I cried. I cried for what seemed like a while in the hospital. It was another wave of feelings crashing over me. Maybe it was the realization of where I was, maybe it was a mixture of hope and despair that this procedure brought, but all I wanted was to be home. Of course, being starving after a day of not eating in preparation for the anesthesia, we took advantage of being in Farmington and stopped at Shake Shack, my favorite burger place. My sore throat was soothed by a chocolate shake all the way home. I went to my parents so they could stay with me until Kevin came from work to pick me up. It was a quiet ride home. My feelings had left my body in the form of those tears cried at the hospital, and now all I felt was numb.

I was expecting similar side effects as a D&C after my hysteroscopy. I spent the next few days working through cramping and discomfort, trying to focus on the fact that something had been found in our quest to determine what was going on and that we were able to have it corrected. I was also wrestling feelings of anger. I was angry that it took three miscarriages to see Dr. Grow and that my ob-gyn hadn't seen my septate uterus sooner. If this had been found earlier, maybe we could have spared ourselves one of our losses and not had to go through that despair again. I tried to be rational, in that mistakes happen and things are overlooked. The problem was that this was much too personal an issue, and so being rationale was much more difficult.

We were told that we would have to wait two months for my body to fully heal before we could begin trying again. I used my app medley to ensure we were being safe and eliminating the chance for me to conceive during those two months. Then the month we were waiting for finally came. It was November, and we had the official okay to begin trying—that is, if we were ready. I had mixed feelings about trying again right away. It had only been three months since our last loss, and I didn't know if I was really ready again. The other nagging part of me wanted to keep pushing. I was only getting older and was fearful that if too much time passed, I would start to change my mind about wanting to push forward. Just as we had decided to try, I received news of my half-sister's passing in New Jersey. I was overcome with so many emotions—sadness for the relationship we didn't have, anger that her life was lost too soon, and heartbreak for the children and grandchildren she left behind. It was a difficult time for my family, and so the furthest thing from my mind was trying to start one of my own. I attended the service with my parents and focused on being there for my dad. This was the second daughter he had lost, and my heart broke for him and all the thoughts of regret I knew he was having.

There is nothing like experiencing a death that makes you realize how you want to live. I had spent so many months wishing for my life to end, only to be faced with my sister's tragic passing, knowing she still wanted to live her life while cancer had other plans. I felt selfish but also didn't want to diminish my emotions because they were true. I had experienced a difficult time and had to own my feelings and allow myself to feel them as they came. I felt it was the only way I would ever get over them, by going through them.

It reminds me of one of the yoga instructors I frequent at my friend Kelsey's studio. Her name is Bre. Often Bre talks about sitting with the discomfort and sensation, that instead of moving and shying away, breathe into your discomfort and allow the fresh air to move stagnant energy our body is holding onto. This was somewhat of a miraculous thought for me. I felt this when she said it. I felt it my heart, my mind, my spirit, and my physical body. I channeled all of my energy and breathe into the parts of myself that felt hard, the parts of myself that have been strong in storing all the trauma I have experienced. I responded to this so much that I felt a desire to pursue a yin workshop she was hosting, and it was the best decision I made. That September Saturday I spent two hours in a passive yoga class, where I felt my body physically release stress. I allowed my body to relax into the postures with her voice as guidance and experienced a level of inner focus that was new to me. I almost felt that I was moving in slow motion after the class, like my body movement was matching the peace I felt within. I am forever grateful for Kelsey and Bre. They have given me more support than they realize through their classes. Most of all it was a time just for me, a time I set aside as important, a time to take care of myself, and that is just what I was doing.

October came and went, this being a pivotal month for me as I finally got the courage to begin writing this book, something I had spent months thinking about. I felt a new sense of relief and therapy from expressing myself through writing. I found it hard to believe how easily it came. From the moment I sat at the computer, it was as if my body was taken over and the words just flowed from me. I would sit at the computer for hours, feeling like if I stopped, I might not be able to start again. I wrote like that for just over a week or so, before receiving the news of my half-sister's passing. I didn't feel like writing anymore, and so I stopped for some time.

November came and went, and it felt odd to begin celebrating the holiday seasons again. Thanksgiving Day was peaceful. Kevin's team won the big game against our crosstown rival, and we spent the day with both of our immediate families. The following weekend was my mother's birthday, and so we treated her to a nice dinner at her restaurant of choice. I wanted to enjoy the time with my family but felt so preoccupied at the time. Despite my best efforts, I just wasn't feeling myself but I don't know if it showed.

I remember us getting our Christmas tree the weekend after Thanksgiving. It was the earliest that we had ever gotten our tree, and I was looking forward to enjoying the decorations for a bit longer this year. Kevin knows how happy the holiday decor makes me, and so I am sure that was part of his motivation to get things rolling. I am glad that we did. It was a welcome distraction to decorate our home and begin planning for the upcoming festivities. There is something about the holidays that I love, and I know many people agree (and disagree) about the feelings you get this time of year. For me at least, I feel happier, a bit nostalgic, and always look forward to gift giving and lots of good food.

I was ahead in terms of my shopping list, something that never happens, and Kevin was on his way to a playoff game, one game away from the state championship that he's had his eye on since he accepted the head coaching job at MHS. We were feeling pretty good and starting to be a bit more optimistic about the future. We both convinced ourselves that our troubles were behind us. We believed that my last procedure had corrected our issue, and now we just had to beat the typical miscarriage rate of 10–20 percent, which in my mind is still rather high, but it was much better than my previous 80 percent failure rate. And so, on a cold winter night next to our fire, we conceived our fourth child under the Christmas tree.

It was strange in that I didn't think I was pregnant, even though I knew we had sex during my ovulation. I didn't take a test. I was trying to be more lax this time around and not stress myself out so much. And so I waited until the first day of my missed period to take a test. It turned positive immediately. Kevin was a little down from his season ending one game too early, and so I thought the positive test could be a great way to pick him up. I secretly grabbed some tissue paper and a small gift bag and placed the positive test inside. I brought him the gift and insisted he open one present early to get in the spirit. I was right. As soon as he saw the test he was elated, and so was I. I even got the opportunity to make it a better experience for him this time around, a small gift to open seemed a little better than blurting it out in the kitchen on a Tuesday as I had done in the past. This time around would be different.

Since we got the news just a few days before Christmas, we opted to wait until after the New Year to contact the doctor for an office visit. I was a bit anxious as you can imagine, and so I called before the New Year and was able to get an appointment for Friday, January 3. Kevin attended the appointment with me, that included both blood work and an ultrasound. Dr. Grow wasn't available that day, and so a nurse in the office performed the ultrasound. Kevin and I waited anxiously. This was a big moment for us. The last two ultrasounds we experienced ended with the worst news imaginable. This time we prayed for a heartbeat and good news.

This initial appointment was anxiety ridden although we both did our best to appear calm for each other. As the nurse began the exam, she affectionately called our baby a little bean as she pointed out features on the monitor. Then the moment we were waiting for. We were able to hear the heartbeat and see a small flicker. We were elated when we were able to hear our baby's heartbeat, a luxury we had not realized with our first three pregnancies. To say that we both breathed a sigh of relief is an understatement. We held hands, exchanged smiles of relief, and I held back a few tears that wanted to stream down my cheek. I could see the relief and joy on Kevin's face as well. Maybe our troubled roads really were behind us. Maybe, just maybe, the hysteroscopy was just what I needed to finally conceive a child of our very own. We left the office on cloud nine, holding our first ultrasound photo in our hands, excited to be able to share the news with our parents.

They confirmed I was six weeks along and everything looked great. My HCG levels were the highest that they had ever been at 44,000. The growth rate of the baby was right on track with six weeks, and everything looked great. It was the best feeling leaving the office that day. We booked a follow-up appointment with Dr. Grow in two weeks on our way out, with our very first ultrasound photo in hand. As much as I didn't want to believe that my septate uterus was the cause of our losses, mostly in part because of how minor it appeared to be, I was willing to place the blame there given our new positive results. Honestly, I really just wanted to put all of those bad memories behind us and enjoy the present moment we were in.

We had our first Social Sabby Sunday's group session the following week, followed by dinner at my in-laws to share the news. We were still very hesitant to share the news with others as I was only six weeks, and so we opted to keep it to our parents for the time being, along with my brother and sister-in-law who we knew would also be at the family dinner that day. I shared tears of joy with my mother-in-law and excitement with the rest of the family, and it was a nice feeling to be able to share our good news with those around us. On one hand I remember not wanting to tell anyone based on our previous experiences. On the other hand, I no longer wanted to deny myself the opportunity to celebrate the life growing inside of me. I had done that too many times before. They were especially excited when we shared the photo and news received from the doctor's office. We shared that we would keep them posted as we had our next few appointments and were on our way. I remember sharing the news with my parents that same night. We stopped by on our way home to share our ultrasound photo and were met with the same joyous reactions. They, along with my in-laws, had shared in our previous losses;

and so they were as excited as we were to hear the news of a heartbeat. They were excited as we imagined them to be, my mother crying and Dad giving Kevin a big hug and congratulations. Something I have realized about my dad is that few things bring him joy the way a baby does. I watched him with my sisters' children, and it was always heartwarming to see a man, who is typically very reserved and stoic, laugh and play and speak in baby talk. He hugged me and told me that our child would learn to swim in their pool the way my nephew and nieces had, and I was grateful for that upcoming opportunity. I was grateful for his excitement. I was grateful to share our happiness with them, but also felt joy thinking of all the memories to come and being able to experience them together as a family. We didn't stay long as a result of my first trimester symptoms in full swing, exhaustion and nausea being at the top of the list. We said our good-byes and promised to share updates with our upcoming appointment.

The next two weeks seemed to fly by, and before I knew it, it was time to go back to UConn. This time around surely felt different than the last three. I was in a better place mentally, and the physical symptoms I was experiencing were pacifying in a way. I was experiencing all-day nausea, the kind that is always present and sometimes goes away in fleeting moments. My body ached and the level of fatigue I felt was unmatched to date. I found myself crawling into bed sometimes as early as 8:00 p.m., only to find myself dragging in the morning, despite setting my alarm hours later. I would pull myself from bed by 9:00 or 10:00 a.m., only to feel the need to nap a few short hours later. I did not feel guilty one bit for giving myself what my body was craving, rest. I began doing less at home, and Kevin picked up all of my slack. We ate out more when I wasn't feeling up to cooking, or Kevin and I would make something together, a bit of a lesson for future months when I knew I would need his help even more in the kitchen, a task I usually enjoyed independently.

Every ache and pain brought me joy, I was grateful to be nauseous every day and feel lethargic at times because I knew it meant by body was doing what it should. It was working hard to create our little bean.

January 16 seemed to arrive in the blink of an eye. It was the first time we would be meeting with Dr. Grow at UConn since our positive result, since a nurse in the office had conducted our first ultrasound earlier in the month. The appointment could not have gone better. In fact, Kevin and I were reassured and even a bit surprised by his reactions and how confident he appeared to be in our progress to date. It was nothing but good news all around. We not only heard the heartbeat for the second time, we were amazed to see how much growth had transpired in only two weeks. The baby was physically so much bigger. The measurements were right on track for eight weeks. My levels were on the mark. It seemed too good to be true. We could see more of the baby's body shape, the enlarged head and also the small black dots that would become their eyes. My blood work levels were right on track, and I was measuring at eight weeks. Everything about the exam was on the mark. Then we received the news from Dr. Grow that he was so confident in our progress that he recommended I begin seeing my regular gynecologist. He assured us that he and his office would be available for anything we needed along the way, but that at that point there was no real need to continue with our specialty office visits. He shared that couples in the past had come in for bimonthly checkups, and that we could do that as well if it would help to settle us or alleviate any concerns. If that wasn't something we were interested in pursuing, then I could contact my primary ob-gyn to begin setting up my appointments and checkups with her. We hugged, thanked him for all of his help along the way, and left the office with a renewed and strengthened confidence that this time around things would be different for us. It was Thursday January 16, 2020, and we couldn't have been any further from the impending truth that lay less than two weeks away.

The following day I called my ob-gyn to schedule my first appointment with her. I was hoping for another two weeks so that I would be at the ten-week mark, but her first available was a few days shy of that, and happened to be on my birthday, so I decided to take it. I had already planned to have a day of self-care. I was turning thirty-five, and for me, there is nothing like a fresh haircut and manicure to put a little pep in my step. I had dinner plans with my husband to try a restaurant we'd been talking about for literally over a year, and I was excited to get the day started with a fresh photo of our little bean.

Chapter 6

Today is January 30, 2020, and it is 4:53 a.m. I finally decided that I had lain in bed long enough to realize I was not going to fall back asleep anytime soon. There are simply too many thoughts racing through my mind, and maybe if I get them down on paper, I can get some rest in a few hours. I've become quite a light sleeper over the last several years. It's quite a departure from the heavy sleeper I once was, when I could be knocked out for ten to twelve hours straight without a problem. Now it didn't take much to wake me, and tonight was no exception. I woke up as I realized Kevin was having a nightmare. I awoke before him and tried to sooth him back to bed before getting up for a glass of water and to use the bathroom. I was relieved to see that my body was not hemorrhaging from the D&E procedure I had undergone less than nine hours prior. The year 2020 certainly was not shaping up to be the year I had hoped for.

I was nine weeks and one day pregnant with my fourth child when I experienced my second missed miscarriage, as my second and third losses happened naturally at home. There is a certain feeling of restlessness and disbelief when your body doesn't recognize what is happening. It makes it harder to believe because there is nothing to see for yourself. I didn't have the luxury of finding out the news until a few days later on the morning of my thirty-fifth birthday. It certainly was not the day I had planned for myself.

Kevin and I had been so hopeful this time around, cautiously optimistic but optimistic nonetheless. I remember getting the positive pregnancy results on Saturday, December 21, just a few days shy of the Christmas holiday. I remember chuckling when I shared with Kevin that I knew the exact moment we conceived, certainly a memory we would treasure for years to come. This news, well, it was certainly the best gift we could have received. This just a few days after we had received the news that Social Sabby had been awarded a $5,000 grant from The Meriden Foundation, it felt like our luck was finally turning around, and it couldn't have been received at a better time. It was the best way we could have put an end to a tough year we were looking forward to putting behind us.

For obvious reasons we had no intention of sharing the news just yet. We needed some confirmation from our doctor's office. The thing was, with holiday celebrations looming, I was anxious about keeping the news close to our chest as we desired. I had a girl's night planned the evening we found out, and so I swiftly made a trip to the package store (as I learned we call liquor stores in Connecticut after having New York friends give me strange looks when using this terminology years ago in college). I purchased nonalcoholic IPAs. I was excited to find a tool I could use during my girl's night in to keep our secret for now.

I was successful in hiding my beverages with the help of Kevin's YETI metal koozie, along with being the host and insisting I pour shots for my guests. I filled glasses in the other room, hidden from my friends who had no clue my glass was filled with water. This may sound strange, but I was relieved to sincerely enjoy my time with these two friends despite being sober. I must admit that, although many would describe me as outgoing and talkative, I am actually, in fact, a true introvert. I realized this a few years prior when taking one of those tests and understanding that the definition is not the ability to be social or hold a conversation but rather how your energy is impacted from social engagements. It actually made a lot of sense to me once I had the results. I often found myself suffering from social anxiety, sometimes the hardest thing for me to do was engage in small talk, and so many times I relied on an alcoholic beverage or two in social settings to relax and make the process easier for myself. I believe the official term used here is *liquid courage*.

The events from the last year and a half certainly triggered the start of my abuse of alcohol, something I was determined not to repeat. This pregnancy was surely all the motivation I needed, and for the first time I considered and yearned for a life without it, even after the baby was here. It somehow felt so insignificant and unnecessary, a reflection of the mother I wanted to be and the example I wanted to set for my unborn child. I simply wanted to be the best version of myself. It was a great feeling to know that I was able to put that dark time behind me, but also that I had zero desire to drink. It was a far cry from the months prior where sometimes it felt like my only resolve, to escape the endless thoughts cycling through my brain. It was also reassuring that I was able to be social and genuinely enjoy myself without it. It was a testament to this new place in my life, but also the relationships I now choose to surround myself with, those that I felt were sincere and brought me a feeling of nothing but positive energy.

Our secret stayed with us through holiday family gatherings. It was actually easier than I thought, although I hated the little white lies, but of course, it was for good reason. That is, until NYE came and Kevin and I had plans to have dinner with friends and celebrate the ball drop at their house with some additional guests they had invited over. There would be no crowds to hide my lack of drink with just the four of us, and we knew they would be suspicious, and also recommending shots to commemorate the New Year. On the short drive to their home in Middletown, alcohol-free beer in tow, we decided to share the news. To be honest, it was a bit of a relief to share our news and say it aloud to someone other than each other. Pito was one of Kevin's best childhood friends; and his fiancé, Taylor, that I had met recently, well, we became instant friends. You know when you meet someone and you just click? That is how it was with Taylor. In the short time we knew each other we had gone on two overnight trips, one to Boston for Kevin's birthday and another to Newport at the end of the summer. Kevin often joked that if he didn't know any better, he would have thought we had been life-long friends. It was refreshing to meet someone new and automatically know that it was a friendship that would last. We both shared intimate feelings and experiences with each other early on in our friendship, and it felt so natural. We both shared our feelings of our friendship being one that would last, and it was nice to know that I could make new meaningful relationships well into my thirties. I think I always had the incorrect assumption that friends are made in youth, maybe the mantra "no new friends" reinforced that. Maybe it was simply my introverted nature that made me feel a bit hindered in forging new relationships. This may have been part of the reason I had held on to friendships well past their expiration date, something I committed to no longer doing in the new year.

Given this comfort level Kevin and I had, we decided to share the news on New Year's Eve, and they couldn't have been happier for us. They were also excited to have an official designated driver for the night's festivities and the next several months for that matter. We all shared a laugh about that as we talked about our plans and upcoming appointments as Taylor rubbed my belly. It was a significant night of endings for 2019 and hopeful beginnings for the 2020 year ahead.

I remember having dinner plans with girlfriends that Friday night in January after meeting with Dr. Grow and having the confidence to begin sharing our news with those closest to us. They were aware of the struggles we had faced over the last year and a half and also knew that we had begun trying to conceive again, so they were a bit suspicious when I scheduled the dinner. My increased appetite left little to the imagination as I contemplated ordering everything on the menu, and they asked if I had news to share before I even brought the subject up. I was elated to pull my most recent ultrasound photo out of my coat pocket where you could visibly see our baby's features. You could easily see the dark spots on their face where the baby's eyes were beginning to develop, along with the start of arms and legs. It was the furthest along I had ever been, and I could hardly contain my excitement.

The reaction from my friends was heartwarming. They had known how much of a struggle this process had been, and their excitement was palpable. The conversation quickly changed to all things baby, as one of my friends at the table was pregnant with her second child, a baby boy due July 4. We talked about upcoming play dates, and she gave me a few tips she had gained during her first year with her daughter. To say the conversation felt like a surreal dream after the nightmare that had been our lives for the last year and a half would be an accurate reflection of my feelings at that moment. We said our good-byes with extra-long hugs, and I was filled with love for not only this growing child that we looked forward to welcoming later in August, but also for the support and happiness from my friends. It was becoming real, and I allowed myself to really start to get excited.

I was about a week and a half away from my checkup with Dr. Taylor, and I surprised myself with how much I let myself begin to plan. I hadn't even thought of nursery planning or any other baby related things in a long time. I began looking on Pinterest for jungle-themed nurseries, something I always thought was such a cute gender-neutral theme. I began adding pins to a secret board that had been dormant for a year, and it felt good to be excited again. I started searching for random pregnancy-related subjects online and the power of online targeted marketing quickly kicked in. I found myself sending screenshots of the cutest baby outfits during the day to Kevin, and even beginning to think of maternity clothing I would need in the coming months. Despite only being just over two months along, my body was beginning to show the signs of our growing bean.

I couldn't believe just how much and how quickly my body had started to change. Yes, I had experienced some of these symptoms with my prior pregnancies, but not like this. This time around my symptoms were becoming visible to the eye and not just internally felt by me. My belly began taking shape and started to become firmer. My breasts began to grow so much that I felt my bras fit me differently. It was really happening, and I loved every moment of it.

It was Saturday January 25, and Kevin had his end-of-the-year football banquet that afternoon. We were at the school early that morning, organizing final touches for the festivities, and were met by the booster club shortly after our arrival that began setting up decorations in the school cafeteria. To say I was grateful for the best booster club to date to help with the setup and decorating, a task that years prior had fallen on Kevin's and my shoulders, is a severe understatement. My exhaustion was in full gear, and I noticed a stark difference in my energy levels. I was simply not able to complete the number of tasks I once was able to easily or have the stamina I was used to. I was also committed to a new perspective of self-care and not feeling guilty for not pushing myself. My number one priority was to ensure that I was giving myself and my unborn child what we needed, and many times that was rest. I was reveling in my earlier bedtimes coupled with afternoon naps. I felt a sense of luxury for being unemployed and almost felt that it was divine intervention in a way, in that my unemployment allowed me to rest when I needed it, regardless of the time of day it was.

Now I know that I am not responsible for our losses, but I couldn't help but think that in the past maybe work-related stressors had an impact on my ability to carry full term. Even though I know this is not true, I was still grateful to have this new flexible schedule that allowed me to give myself whatever it was that I needed.

The banquet was a great success, and I know that Kevin was relieved it went well and was looking forward to moving on to the next thing. We had our annual Vermont trip to look forward to for Super Bowl weekend, and we both needed the time away. We also looked forward to celebrating our news, my birthday, and our friend Andy's birthday, which is just a few days after mine, in less than a week. We also looked forward to spending time with their children: George, who was so grown-up and talking so much more, and Lena, who was seven months old.

I had one more event for the busy weekend before being able to take it easy and enjoy hitting the thirty-five-year mark later in the week. Being pregnant and being confident in my pregnancy, despite still having reservations for being in my first trimester, certainly made the age easier to celebrate. I was finally realizing our dreams of becoming parents.

That Sunday after the banquet, we held our Social Sabby group session. Afterwards, I attended a baby shower held for my sister. She is expecting her fourth child. To say I was surprised when learning of my sister's pregnancy in the fall probably underestimates how I felt at the moment. I have to be honest in sharing that it was a big pill to swallow. She is five years my senior and became a mother early in her life when I was just fourteen years old. She has been blessed with three children to date: my nephew and godson Julian, who is twenty; my niece Natalia, who is seventeen; and Gia, who is ten. She shared her pregnancy with me via a text which felt impersonal, and it was just so hard to believe. I happened to be out to dinner with a friend who received a similar text from her around the same time. She had said so many times before that she was done having children, even teasing me over the years that while she was almost finished raising her children and looking forward to enjoying more freedom, I would just be starting. That she wasn't envious of the long sleepless nights, even wishing me "good luck" as I embarked on this journey, again and again.

While I was happy for her and I realize that her pregnancy is not about me, but to say that it felt like it couldn't have come at worse timing for the place I was in my life, well, truer words have never been spoken. Our relationship wasn't as close as it had been in the past, and this certainly did not make me feel closer to her. In fact, it made me feel isolated from her. I realize some may perceive that as me being selfish, and I must admit that rereading these words after the fact made me question whether or not I should remove it and what follows. I almost did until I realized that the feelings and thoughts I had in these moments are my truth, and the point of sharing this story is so that others who might have felt this way in their relationships too can know that they are not alone. My intention is never to hurt anyone by sharing my story; in fact, it's the exact opposite. The reality is that I had been in self-preservation mode for a long time. I had come to the realization that my needs, well-being, and mental health had to be my priority. My mental health had to be more important than anyone else's, even my pregnant sister or my mother for that matter.

I was a bit stressed in attending her shower. Most of all, I think I didn't really feel welcome. Let me explain. Attending a baby shower after suffering a miscarriage is a *very* difficult thing for any woman to do, let alone these special circumstances. Friends I had known since middle and high school that my sister had forged relationships with a few years prior had offered to throw her the shower, something I learned a few days before receiving an invitation in the mail. I was hurt that those I considered friends did not feel the need to reach out to include me as they planned a shower for my own sister, and it made me feel that they were not really my friends at all.

It was scheduled two days before my birthday, and I remember feeling disappointed that this celebration was scheduled on my birthday weekend, not because it ruined any plans I had, but because it made me feel that those planning had no consideration of me or the very difficult time I was going through.

Attending a baby shower for your sister that you weren't involved in (not by choice) felt so incredibly insensitive. Were there really no other weekends this could have been scheduled? Why was I finding myself in a position to attend a celebration of my sister's pregnancy after suffering three miscarriages as I reached the official age of geriatric pregnancy? There have been times over the years where I was made to feel that I didn't do enough or wasn't present enough as a friend or sister even while living in another state; it always felt to me that I was held to a higher standard or rather that I never lived up to other's expectations, and it always left me feeling bad about myself. Why didn't I do enough during someone else's special time or hardship, yet I found myself alone when I needed support and was leaning over the edge of the cliff of life? It makes me feel that if the shoe was on the other foot, I would never be forgiven, but I continue to find myself on the receiving end of responsibility for why my relationships with some aren't better than they are, and it was beyond comprehension for me.

Looking back I wonder if they thought they were doing me a favor by saving me the trouble of being involved, knowing I had suffered miscarriages. Or if it's simply a reflection of them not knowing what to say, like most human encounters I have had throughout this experience. I sometimes feel that the biggest opportunity for me through all of this is educating those that haven't experienced it. Somehow trying to get them to understand above all, what *not* to say or do, because quite frankly I feel like I have been through it all at this point. Despite my negative feelings surrounding not being included, I attended the shower for my sister, and myself. My sister seemed appreciative I was there, at least she shared that with me as I was leaving. But it was hard to ignore what felt like stares from some of the invited guests throughout the afternoon. It certainly didn't help the unwanted feelings I felt before arrival. True or not, I felt like some were judgmental about my lack of involvement throughout the process, which was infuriating to feel while I was and still am in mourning even today. I would imagine that most would agree that in this circumstance, they wouldn't have any expectations of a grieving mother who lost an earth side "living" child, so why was I left with this feeling of expectation? I had lost three children, and some didn't even acknowledge it; it is mind boggling to me. For me it highlights how significant the lack of understanding is surrounding this experience. For the first time in my life I didn't care what others thought of me. I finally realized that other's perceptions of me are not my responsibility, and quite frankly, I have no desire to justify myself or share my side of the story. It just doesn't matter to me anymore.

I opted to not obsess over this event as I would have done in the past. I was focused on processing my emotions in a more positive manner so as not to physically impact me the way I felt it had before, sometimes feeling my anger, hurt, or disappointment in the pit of my stomach. Now I had something there much too precious to protect, and so I pushed it from my mind to focus on all the things Kevin and I were looking forward to. Certainly, there was a lot on that list.

My appointment with Dr. Taylor was scheduled for 9:00 a.m., certainly earlier than I was accustomed to being out and about, but it was for good reason. I also had a few errands I planned to run afterwards—some shopping before allowing myself to indulge in a mani/pedi at my favorite nail salon, along with a haircut by Taylor and a lunch visit from Kevin at home. He texted me as I waited in the office lobby that he was going to bring me lunch as a birthday treat, and I knew what it was without him telling me. He said he wanted to treat me to my favorite things for the day, and so I knew that my favorite lobster roll from a local restaurant down the street from our home was in my future. This was certainly a welcomed summer treat to brighten up my cold winter birthday.

I remember telling Kevin that he didn't have to come with me to the appointment. We had received such favorable news from our fertility doctor that it felt routine. I sent him a message as I waited to be called in that I was excited to see how much our bean had grown and that I hoped I would receive a new ultrasound photo so we could compare the growth from our two previous photos. I was greeted happily by Dr. Taylor who shared she was excited when seeing my name on the schedule. She too knew of our struggles in trying to conceive, and it had been sometime since last seeing her before our switch to CARS.

We began the ultrasound, this time being over my belly. She apologized for the older equipment she was using, sharing that they were actually waiting for a new ultrasound machine to arrive and that she didn't like using it. She shared that she was having a hard time picking up the heartbeat and opted for an internal ultrasound, which I was happy to have. Never in a million years would I have expected the news she was about to share. As she began the internal ultrasound, I could quickly see how much the baby had grown. The babies' head was so much larger than the last time we viewed them on screen, and I could see their tiny hands and feet. At that moment I had zero concern that something was wrong. I just assumed it was taking her a minute to find the heartbeat, which was reinforced by her physically hitting the machine on its side for it to work. Clearly, it was outdated technology and a stark difference from our first two ultrasound experiences.

I also had renewed confidence from a gift received by my friend Alyson a few days prior. She was so excited for Kevin and I that she ordered us an at-home ultrasound monitor so that we could listen to the heartbeat at home. A luxury we enjoyed just two days prior. Kevin and I laughed at his skepticism at first hearing the sound, that he insisted we put it on his stomach to make sure it wasn't a fluke. He quickly realized it was legit, and we marveled at the ability to enjoy this in the comfort of our home. I was so grateful for that thoughtful gift. She knew we were still cautious and thought being able to hear our baby anytime we wanted would bring reassurance. She was right.

Here I was lying on the table, to only hear the fateful words again, "I am not finding a heartbeat." I didn't believe her, even questioning if the machine was to blame. I mean, she was hitting it on its side to work for goodness sake. My confidence in her diagnosis was lacking and clearly visible to her. She suggested calling down to the radiology department for an emergency ultrasound to confirm, and of course, I accepted. At that moment I was grateful that the appointment was located in her office that happened to be in our local hospital instead of her other location one town away.

Since I didn't have an appointment and they were squeezing me in, she shared there may be a bit of a wait. At that moment I couldn't care less about wait time, I was eager to have someone confirm what I wanted to believe, what I felt true in my heart, that she was wrong. I mean, we had just heard the heartbeat two days prior Sunday evening at home. How was this possible not even forty-eight hours later? I wrestled with whether or not to text Kevin. He was at work, and I didn't want him to worry unnecessarily. I changed my mind as her office gave me a sheet of paper to bring downstairs to radiology, where the diagnosis read, "Missed miscarriage." The reality is that even though I told him not to come, I needed him there with me.

He immediately called me, and the concern was so apparent in his voice that it automatically put me in a position where I felt I needed to be strong. Even to this day I am so grateful that these tragedies we have faced together in our marriage has made us that much stronger. We have a habit of switching on and off being strong for one another, and I knew I had to be strong at this moment for him. I wasn't convinced yet that we had lost the baby. Kevin met me in the waiting area shortly after we finished our phone call. I filled him in on my experience, stating that I didn't believe it and needed someone else to tell me the same thing.

A few moments later we were called in by someone who appeared very young. I was a bit surprised by how young she seemed and that she would be performing the ultrasound. I told myself to dismiss this, convincing myself she must be qualified in order to perform the exam and maybe she was older than she appeared. My concerns on her abilities were heightened by the amount of discomfort

I experienced during the exam. She, in my opinion, clearly did not have a lot of experience based on how the next fifteen minutes went. After what felt like an eternity, I asked if she was seeing a heartbeat as Kevin loomed over her shoulder. At that moment, I was even more happy that he was there and could see the screen that was facing away from me. She replied that she was not able to answer any questions and that we would have to return to Dr. Taylor's office upstairs to receive the results.

Two hours after my initial appointment time, we found ourselves waiting in a room to receive the results. It was all too familiar, but I held on to a glimmer of hope while also preparing myself for bad news. Kevin and I both felt that we heard a heartbeat just a few moments prior, so I used that to tell myself it wasn't over yet. We waited for twenty minutes, and our anger began to build. Finally, she arrived in the room and the expression on her face told us the news before she could utter the words. I was in shock. Both of our heads dropped in disbelief, and at that moment I wanted to be anywhere other than in that office.

It was a sick déjà vu of our first three pregnancies. Somehow, I feel like the news wasn't really hitting me. We spoke for a few minutes, and the conversation quickly changed to our options, all the things I had heard before and didn't want to hear again. I almost wanted to stop her, saying this is not my first rodeo. I am aware of the nightmare that follows, and I do not want to discuss it. I do not want to be around another living soul other than my husband, whose arms I ached to be in. I needed to try to process this again, alone. She told us she didn't need the room for any other appointments and to take as long as we needed. She also shared that she would contact Dr. Grow to share the news and that we could decide to proceed with either office of our choosing.

As soon as the door closed, we broke down. I don't think I have ever witnessed Kevin cry the way he did in the office that morning. We held each other close, hugging each other so tight but somehow not tight enough. We were devastated, and angry, and just kept saying how unfair this was. We both agreed that we needed to get in touch with Dr. Grow, but first needed to compose ourselves to get home. I was sad that we had driven ourselves separately and had to each make the drive alone, although I was behind him the entire way home.

I felt sick to my stomach, mixed with hunger pains from not eating anything yet, but eating was the furthest thing from my mind. I made myself a cup of ginger tea as I began to put away our groceries that had been delivered earlier in the morning. I remember picking the delivery time the night before, assuming I'd be back from my appointment at least an hour before they were scheduled to arrive. Back when I still believed that I was pregnant and had hope for our looming future of parenthood. I sat at the kitchen table in silence for a while, just staring at the floor, or table, or blank wall unable to gather my thoughts. I felt nothing. I cried but not like before. I was in disbelief.

I recall reading something online last week that spoke about our body's ability to protect us from trauma, that our physical body can actually store the trauma until we are able to process it. I felt like that was happening to me. I felt that if I allowed myself to really absorb the reality of the situation that I mentally and emotionally just couldn't handle it. Even now as I write this and know it's over, again, I feel nothing. I feel numb.

The phone rang and it was the second call from my mother. I knew I couldn't ignore it any longer, but I just didn't have the strength to tell her. Verbalizing the words aloud would make it too real. Bless Kevin's heart for answering the call and giving her the news. She was on speaker phone, and I almost wished she wasn't, based on her reaction. In my thirty-five years of life, I have never heard my mother cry the way she did when Kevin told her. She sobbed uncontrollably, and it was almost too much to bear. I was trying so hard to keep it together for myself and for Kevin. I didn't have it in me to be strong for anyone else.

Ultimately, I joined the conversation but kept it short because I wasn't in a place to talk. I told her I planned to rest and would call her later. Kevin had called his parents to share the news on his way home from the hospital and was greeted with the same reactions, understandably. Our parents knew of our struggles and experienced them with us. They were hurting too. I also texted Taylor to share the news since I had a haircut appointment with her later that afternoon that I knew I could not make. She was gracious, shared her condolences, and offered support with anything we needed, something I appreciated in the moment.

Now that we had overcome the herculean task of telling our parents, Kevin immediately called CARS and left a message for Dr. Grow. After hanging up the phone, he shared his disappointment with me, making the appointment on my birthday, and frankly so did I. We both never would have dreamed this would happen again, and now this memory will forever be tied to something that should be a happy occasion. The reality is though, that regardless of when the appointment had been made, the outcome would not have been any different, as much as we wanted it to be. He ordered lobster rolls for pick-up, even though I didn't think I could eat. The reality was that we needed to put something in our system, and clearly, I was not cooking anything. It was a struggle to simply be awake and sit with this information.

We both ate and decided to try to take a nap. We both needed a break from the news we received just hours before. Kevin was able to fall asleep, but I was restless, so I lay there for hours staring at the ceiling, feeling more and more sick with every moment that passed. I couldn't accept this. I didn't want to believe it. I felt exhausted. I knew what lay ahead of us, and I didn't want to have to go through this again. I didn't want to have another procedure. I didn't want another disappointment. As I lay there with this myriad of thoughts swirling in my brain, lying there feeling numb, there were several loud knocks followed by our doorbell. I immediately felt my entire body get hot with anger. Who the hell decided to show up at my house on the worst day of my life? It was my mother and father. Despite my specific request to not come to my home, to not call me, they came anyway, and I didn't answer the door. I was angry but more so baffled. Why was it that my mom was unable to accept what I communicated at face value? Why was it that the one person who always seemed to know what to do or what to say, all of sudden had no boundaries and made me feel worse with pressing and incessant questions about our losses, or when we planned to start again? Would you ask someone that almost died in a car crash when they are going to start driving again? It felt like no matter how much I communicated how hurtful these questions were, they would subside for a short time only to return, again and again. It was almost as if, as soon I started trying to become a mother, she stopped knowing how to mother me. I remember calling her later that day and communicating that my needs were more important than her wanting to console me. As direct as I felt I was, even today I am still faced with her bringing up this topic that I clearly have removed from the table. I even recall asking Kevin if he was okay with me telling her that we decided to not have children, just so she wouldn't keep talking to me about it. I am still entertaining that idea. I mean, I even wrote a whole book about my feelings, and how dark some of my days have been, and let her read it, hoping it would shine a light on how to best provide support for me, hoping it would make a difference; it didn't. Unfortunately, this was the case with many people in my life. Somehow it has been most hurtful with my mom though, and I think the reason why is that it has been such a stark contrast to all of our other experiences together. I fear that this has impacted our relationship, and she isn't aware of the gravity of it all.

As I lay there that cold January afternoon of my 35th birthday, I felt like a failure again, like less of a woman for not being able to produce a healthy child for my husband and myself. Although we were pretty certain that the news was, in fact, real, we wanted a second opinion and so we awaited a call back from UConn so that we could request a second opinion. Unfortunately, we missed the call and knew we wouldn't be able to get in touch with the office until the following morning. I was so restless. I can only describe it as the feeling you get when you are sick and resting. There comes a point where you begin to feel sicker by resting so much. It's almost like you have to push yourself to get up in hopes that the activity can start to snap your body out of it. This is how I felt Tuesday afternoon. I didn't want to do anything, I didn't want to see anyone, but I couldn't stay in the house for another minute. Kevin woke up, and I asked if he'd be up to go get some ice cream. I just needed to get some fresh air before the sunset and nightfall. I also felt like I was starting to get a fever and welcomed something cold to eat.

The thirty-minute round trip was a welcomed distraction. Clearly, neither of us were up for our dinner plans, and opted for greasy Chinese at home. We ate on the couch and comforted each other by our physical presence but not many words. There was simply nothing else left to say.

As he left for work the next morning, my heart ached for him that he had to work through his sadness but I also tried to reassure myself that it could be beneficial to keep his mind occupied. We were expecting follow-up calls from both doctors' offices and told each other we would reach out as soon as one of us heard back. He received a call from UConn first from our nurse, who shared Dr. Grow would be reaching out to us later in the day. Shortly after I received a call from Dr. Taylor who shared that she had spoken with Dr. Grow yesterday to deliver the news and that he was just as taken aback as we were with the results. She went on to confirm that he shared her recommendation to pursue a D&C and that either office could perform the surgery. I shared it was my preference to proceed with UConn and awaited Dr. Grow's call.

It was already 10:00 a.m., and although I had been up for hours, I was still in bed. I decided it was time to peel myself from under the covers, convincing myself a steaming hot shower would serve me well. It certainly did. The hot water running down my body seemed to wash away the bad news we had received twenty-four hours prior, although nothing in our circumstances had changed. My phone rang just as I was starting to get dressed, and it was Dr. Grow. He immediately shared his condolences and surprise at our news. I shared with him that although we trusted Dr. Taylor's abilities, we would feel more confident in the news if we could have a second opinion. He obliged our request for a third internal ultrasound and said we could come into the office now, as he would only be in until 11:30 a.m. and it was currently ten fifteen. Kevin was planning to stop home around ten thirty, so I told him we would do our best to get there for 11:00 a.m. since we were just under 30 minutes away.

Kevin was glad that we were able to get in, and we rushed to the Farmington office, but not before I made us two bagels at home. I have learned my lesson from the day prior with not eating before my appointment, and not knowing how long we would be there. I needed to get something in my system. We ate in the car on the way to the office, not wanting to miss our opportunity to see Dr. Grow. We arrived at 11:00 a.m., and as we walked into the office, we hoped for the best but had to prepare ourselves for the worst.

A few moments later the news we were hoping to avoid had been confirmed. There had been significant growth since our eight-week appointment, and the monitor showed the form of our baby's body. There was no heartbeat, and the baby measured at nine weeks and one day when I should have been nine weeks and five days. This had just happened in the last few days. We sat in somber silence as Dr. Grow began discussing options with us, at least this time we were better prepared to process the news since we had twenty-four hours to accept this fate. He explained that since I was nine weeks along and due to the baby's size being as large as it was, they would need to perform the procedure in a hospital.

We both expressed that our preference was for him to perform the surgery. I had a higher comfort level in having the procedure at UConn, which was a more advanced facility than our other option, our local hospital. The challenge we now faced was timing. He would be traveling for the next several days, and he would have to check his schedule to see how quickly we could have it performed. He shared it could be as late as a week away, which of course was not ideal for a variety of reasons. Since it was a missed miscarriage and my body was not recognizing the baby loss, there was no telling when nature may begin taking its natural course.

I had experienced my last two losses at home, but was nowhere near the term I was now. I must admit that even though my last loss in August 2019 was six weeks, it was one of the most painful physical experiences of my life. I couldn't imagine how much worse it would be this time around. There was the added concern of needing to capture my baby for genetic testing we were opting for. The thought of being responsible to contain my loss in a sample for evaluation was too much to bear but was a real reality I may have to face. He could see my despair while I gave that scenario thought and asked us to wait in the exam room while he worked to move his schedule around and order additional testing for Kevin and I.

The nurse greeted us, gave her condolences, and began to go over blood work that we could complete while awaiting details around surgery scheduling. These tests would confirm whether or not there were any chromosome abnormalities. In asking for more information on what that could mean, Dr. Grow had explained that sometimes one parent or the other or a combination of the two could result in either duplicate chromosomes or lack of chromosomes needed for healthy baby development. He went on to say that if in fact that was the case, our next course would be to explore IVF. That through the IVF process, they are able to add any missing chromosomes that would be identified through the testing we were about to undergo.

More tests, more unknowns, and more unanswered questions. Just when we thought we had identified our root cause being my septate uterus, we were back to square one. While Kevin and I were both willing to do what it took to find a resolution and move forward with a healthy full-term pregnancy, we both were unsure if another loss was something we could endure. In fact, during the conversation Kevin expressed this very concern, telling the doctor he didn't know if we could go through another loss. Of course, Dr. Grow understood, and the empathy he felt for us at that moment was visible on his face. He expressed that he understood how difficult this has been for us but that he has worked with thousands of couples in our shoes that have gone on to have healthy children and not to lose hope.

We went downstairs to have more blood tests completed. As Kevin awaited his turn and they were finishing up collecting my samples, Dr. Grow appeared. He shared that due to a variety of scheduling conflicts, the soonest and apparent only option would be to have the surgery later that evening. I immediately thought of the bagel I had eaten on the way to the office, concerned this would disqualify me for this option. He said it would be okay and enough time in between, as he didn't think it would be before 7:00 p.m., just not to eat or drink anything else for the remainder of the day before the procedure. At that moment, I have never been so grateful as I was to have eaten that bagel on the way to the appointment.

We were very grateful to Dr. Grow that he was being so accommodating to us, squeezing in the procedure so last minute before his travels. Kevin and I agreed that it was an almost invisible silver lining to the entire situation. So much had changed in twenty-four hours, but at least I didn't have to worry about waiting for nature to take its course or draw out the physical piece of our pain any longer than needed. I just wanted it to be over. It was a far cry from the baby clothing snapshots my phone held from just a few days earlier.

Given the time of day, we were the only ones in the entire surgical area. We arrived at 4:00 p.m. for intake, knowing that we most likely had a few hours ahead of us to wait. Despite being there early, I would have much rather waited at the hospital than at home. In some way it made me feel that things were moving along, and we were closer to a resolution. I have mixed reviews about the staff, but to be honest that was the absolute least of my concern, I had confidence in my doctor and awaited his arrival with Kevin by my side.

I remember being wheeled into the surgery room and having to switch to the operating table. There is something about the bright lights that always makes me feel uneasy before the luxury of nothingness hits with anesthesia. It always makes me feel like a specimen about to be probed. I remember my first D&C and feeling like it was reminiscent of every alien abduction movie scene I have ever seen. I was reminded of this first experience over a year ago as the staff proceeded to get me ready.

One of the last things I remember before waking up in the recovery room was the extreme rush of pain I felt from my IV. I've been put under general anesthesia several times in the past but never have I recalled it being so painful, so quick, and so aggressive. I immediately said something to the nurse, describing extreme heat and sharp pains in my arm. She appeared a bit concerned but said some heat and discomfort was expected, to which I replied, "A warning would have been nice." (Clearly, I hadn't lost my outspoken nature even at this moment). The look on her face told me everything I needed to know, and affirmed my first impression of the anesthesiologist. Clearly, she was not a fan either. She apologized, and soon the pain subsided. An oxygen mask was placed over my mouth, and I was instructed to take deep breaths as the nurse held my right hand and Dr. Grow my left. I remember experiencing the room spinning, the way it does if you have had too much to drink and are trying to gather your bearings by placing a foot on the floor. Only this time around, it was a welcomed fadeaway.

About forty-five minutes later, I woke up in the recovery room with another nurse by my side. I felt pretty out of it, like I was moving in slow motion. My throat felt as dry as a desert, and so she quickly accepted my request for water. The relief from the water made me feel as if it were my first sip of life, slowly bringing me back to it. A few moments later Kevin was there, and my emotions overcame me. I recall this from my last two procedures and had prepared myself for an inability to control my feelings. As strong as I had tried to be, the medicine flowing through my body no longer allowed me to hold back my tears. I grabbed Kevin's hand as they streamed down my face, and I began taking long deep breaths trying to collect myself. A symptom I hadn't recalled from previous surgeries was an uncontrollable shaking of both of my legs. The nurse shared that it was a typical body response to the anesthesia, but it was new to me and a bit concerning. If you have ever experienced violent shaking as a result of being very cold, that is the only way I can really describe the involuntary movement.

I stayed in bed long enough to drink two additional cups of water and begin to gather myself, waiting for the passive leg shaking to stop lengthened this wait time. I asked the nurses to wait on the other side of the curtain once they had detached me from all of the machinery so that Kevin could help me get dressed. I felt like a child, unable to bend over or tie my shoes. At that moment I was so grateful that he was there. As the nurse reviewed my discharge instructions, I resisted the urge to tell her that I already knew it all and let her finish. I simply stayed silent and nodded, especially as she told me to not eat anything heavy as nausea was a side effect of the anesthesia. She recommended I begin with crackers and toast, and that if my stomach could handle that, then I could try heavier foods. She was clearly unaware of my plans for Shake Shack on the way home.

I waited in a wheelchair at the hospital entrance with one of the nurses as Kevin pulled the car around. He helped me get into the car as she wished us well. As soon as he got into the driver's seat and closed the door behind him, he asked if I still wanted Shake Shack, but I had already put the directions on the dash for him. He laughed, and it was good to hear. It may sound ridiculous, but I had made it a new habit of stopping there after a procedure at UConn since it is a short seven-minute drive away, but twenty-five minutes from our home. Sometimes food can be comforting, the way a cup of hot chocolate warms you on a cold winter's day. That coupled with the fact that I hadn't eaten since ten thirty that morning and it was now almost nine o'clock at night, I needed something substantial.

I wasn't able to go inside, and so we decided to take the food to go to eat in the comfort of our home. I sipped my chocolate shake the whole ride home, and it provided some comfort to my sore throat. We sat at the kitchen table where I devoured my mushroom burger and cheese fries. I was grateful for that simple pleasure in that heavy moment. Kevin went to bed before me, exhausted not only from the events from the last two days, but also from being up at 5:00 a.m. for a 6:00 a.m. weightlifting session at school. He unfortunately did not have the same luxury as me who stayed in bed until 10:00 a.m. I told him I would be there in a few minutes. I sat in silence at the kitchen table just as I had the morning prior, slowing finishing my shake.

Although I knew my body needed rest, I felt wide awake. Too much had transpired in the last two days. How would I ever settle my mind to get some rest? I slowly made my way to the bedroom to change my clothes from the long day. I turned on my diffuser with essential oil in hopes that would help me rest, and liberally applied lavender oil on my wrists, neck, behind my ears, and a bit under my nose, anything to try to help me relax.

The night prior I had randomly stumbled upon reruns of *The Fresh Prince of Bel-Air* and fell asleep to the sound of the familiar character voices. It was the episode where Will wears a suit that makes him appear to be 300lbs, and he is spying on his girlfriend Lisa as she shops at the grocery store with her male friend Dana. Surprisingly, it made me laugh, something I hadn't been able to do for a really long time after our other losses. Was I becoming immune to this whole process? I stopped that thought train and allowed myself the chance to get lost in the show in hopes to get some rest. There was something about watching my favorite childhood show, the one that I remember waiting for a new episode each week, that made me relax a bit. As I sit here thinking of it now, maybe it somehow brought me back to a time before all the pain experienced over the last eighteen months. Maybe it allowed me to forget for just a minute about the gravity of the life events that we were undergoing. Regardless of what it was, I needed it again and I found myself searching for episodes. I recorded the series as a future safety net and watched the two episodes available on demand before falling asleep.

It was 3:30 a.m. this morning when I awoke, waking up Kevin from his unpleasant dream. I had hoped my trip to the bathroom and a glass of water would be what I needed to get back to bed. I was sorely wrong but not surprised. I lay in bed for another hour and a half, thinking about writing. The desire to capture the events from the last forty-eight hours grew too strong. I haven't had the opportunity to capture these feelings in real time, something I hoped never to be able to do. I tried getting out of bed slowly, not knowing what time it was or how much longer Kevin had to rest. He, of course, heard me and I told him I couldn't sleep and was going to the office to write. As I sat at my computer, I realized it was almost 5:00 a.m. and that his alarm would be going off soon. I felt badly that I had interrupted the last few moments he had to rest, but I simply couldn't stay in bed any longer.

It is now almost 9:30 a.m., and I have been sitting at this desk for four and a half hours. Suddenly, I feel at a loss for words. I can longer recap the events that have transpired because I am sitting here in real time not knowing what is next. I feel numb. Maybe my body is still protecting me from the truth it knows I can no longer handle. As I fight the thoughts that maybe I am one of the many women who cannot conceive, I try to focus on the fact that I have been able to get pregnant. In fact, each of the four times that we have actively tried, we have been successful. I am grateful for that since I am aware that many couples struggle to conceive. I try to hold on to the fact that my issue is with carrying full term and that there are still outstanding test results that may provide the answers we so desperately seek. The reality though is that I am starting to come to terms with the fact that this may not be in the cards for us.

Kevin overheard me saying that to my mother on the phone last night, and I could see him shaking his head in the kitchen as I lay on the couch. It is a reality he is not ready to face, and I totally understand that. I don't know if it is my logical personality, or my desire to try to prepare myself for news that we might receive one day, or maybe a combination of the two. I do still have hope that we will be parents one day of biological children, but I also must entertain other options available to us to have a family. I have thought of adoption and how wonderful it could be to provide a loving home for a child that is in need of loving parents. Kevin mentioned a surrogate yesterday, and somehow, I found that thought devastating and scary. The idea of having another woman carry my child, although a blessing and miracle and option that has worked for many other couples, just made me sad. It made me feel inadequate as a woman, as a wife. It also immediately made me anxiety ridden, thinking of the fact that you have no control over your child's environment as they are developing in someone else's womb. Not to mention that I have experienced on four occasions the bond that is formed instantly between mother and child. I was not ready to entertain an idea that didn't provide me that experience. That may change as we obtain new information, but I can only express how I feel today, at this moment. It is also twelve hours since my baby has been removed from my body, so maybe it's not the time for me to even think about this, but here I am thinking of it.

I think the reality that I am learning to accept is that we ultimately have no real control over our lives. For a long time, I felt the opposite. If you do the right things, work hard toward your goals, things generally work out in your favor, at least they had for the most part for me. While things didn't always go exactly according to my plan, I certainly felt that for the most part, I had lived the life

I envisioned for myself. Of course, as I have gotten older, my goals and definition of success have changed dramatically for the better. I attribute a lot of those changes to having Kevin in my life, and during these dark moments, I hold on to him closer and thank God that he is in my life. Certainly, I would not have been able to make it through these unexpected experiences while trying to conceive without him, and for that I am extremely grateful.

Maybe this is the life lesson that I am meant to learn, and maybe my life purpose is sharing it with others who are or have experienced similar unfortunate circumstances. I know I have mentioned before the mantra I always believed in but was not actually living according to "Everything happens for a reason." I now think this was a foreshadowing for the life I am living now. I also think it is a small paint stroke in a much bigger picture.

Something I am working to accept is that there is a plan for me and my life, it's just not my plan. Sometimes I can be so rigid in my own plans, desires, and goals that I am failing myself in that I am limiting my potential to my simple human plans. I realize now that the universe has something much bigger in store, and I am learning to flow with the timing of my life. It's the same approach I was forced to take in my career. I realize now why all of those jobs never worked out. Because those bad things that happened that I never planned for set me on the path that I am supposed to be on. I realize now that things happen in time as they are meant to, as hard as that may be to accept on days like today. Days like today when all of my plans are washed away yet again. Days like today when I am working to pick myself up and get through the day's grief instead of planning nurseries and making lists of baby names.

My life lesson through all of this is that I must surrender to it all. I must allow nature's divinity to work its wonderful magic. I must believe that good days are ahead of me. I must allow myself to grieve and give myself whatever it is that I need without feeling guilty, something I have become much better at over the last few months. I now realize that sometimes being productive is getting extra rest, watching TV, and eating in. Sometimes self-care is quality time with family and friends, sometimes it is giving myself the alone time that

I know I need to recharge. Sometimes it is saying no to others so that I can say yes to myself.

At the age of thirty-five, I now have a deeper understanding of what it means to love yourself first. There have been so many other circumstances where I sacrifice my own well-being for the sake of others or to keep the peace in a certain situation at the expense of my own feelings. This is something I am committed to no longer doing, and that provides me with a renewed inner strength that I always knew was there. Through these losses, I have found my voice in sharing my most vulnerable moments and it has made me feel more connected to those around me. It is so amazing how much strength you can find in being vulnerable. It took me a while to get here, but I am so glad to now have this perspective. It is certainly helping me find myself as I travel this lonely road once again.

In my pursuit to find resources online that helped me to get through these hard times, I am grateful for the many spiritual people I have begun to follow. These simple posts aid in daily positive affirmations that lift my spirits. There is one recent Instagram page I began following, @morganharpernichols and I am so glad that I found her page. I am sharing it here in hopes it can provide the same comfort for you as it has for me. Not only are the messages powerful, but they are accompanied by beautiful and serene imagery that I find to be very calming. I want to share two messages that resonated with me yesterday, as I was fighting the urge to dwell in my despair. It was a single post with several messages and images included. One was titled "Pursuit," and it read,

> One day I hope you look back and see that even though the past felt so heavy on your shoulders, you kept breathing deep, you kept going. You did not stop pursuing each new day with hope, because even when you did not have the language for how you were going to make it through, strength was rising up in your bones. And even in the heaviness, you continued to travel beyond the borders. You continued to go

out into new unknowns even though you did not know how everything would come together. This is courage. This is strength. And when you look back, I hope you are able to see it all. (MHN)

My hope is that you too will continue on, despite how dark the days ahead may seem, that one day there will be light and love. That even if you are unable to gather the words today, tomorrow might be different, and that if you can hold on to that hope even in times of despair, you are moving mountains. I hope that you can begin to find the joys in simple everyday pleasures, as I have learned these are the moments to live for. These are the moments to be grateful for, the moments that we will miss most when we are no longer here. My hope is that you give yourself what you need and are okay with the fact that may change day by day, or even hour by hour. I certainly did not picture myself writing today, but I felt compelled to and it is helping me to heal. To share my innermost feelings in hopes it someday reaches someone that needs to hear it fills me with peace and appreciation for finding the strength to share my story. It is okay if you're not okay, but just remember that even though it may not seem like it now, you are getting through this and it will get better. There is no timeline for grief, and the reality is that people do not "get over" losses, you simply learn to live with the pain. I find solace in knowing that one day I will meet my four children, and when I do, it will be the most beautiful reunion. Until that day comes, I surrender to God's plan and know that he has something much more special in store for me than anything I could have imagined or planned for myself.

One final message from the post mentioned above from @morganharpernichols: "You can still know peace without knowing what comes next."

I will hold on to this message as I embark on the months and years ahead, hoping I can remember to surrender to it all. That is the thing about grief. It is not a straight road. Just as you feel you are making progress, the road dips down a steep hill and you find yourself holding on until you reach the bottom of the valley.

It has been just over a week since my last D&E, our fourth loss. In some ways I feel like I am just starting to process the news. My body is still suffering from the side effects of the procedure, but I can't help to wonder if the lethargic feelings I am facing is simply my depression seeping its way back in. I have started having urges to drink again and did over the weekend. It was a welcomed feeling of a bit of relief and ability to relax, a stark cry from the new woman I found myself to be just a few short weeks earlier. It's funny how a single event can change you, how quickly everything can be different. It takes only an instant.

I shared the news with my therapist yesterday, and it felt like déjà vu, only this time I don't even know how to feel. There are simply no words, and I am tired of this being my story. Although I know those reaching out to share support mean well, I don't want to be in the position of receiving condolences again. I don't want to talk about it. I just want it all to go away. I feel that my mind and body are protecting me at this point, protecting me from a truth and loss that I can no longer bear. I felt such a connection to the child growing inside of me that I am now forced to deny in order to protect myself from truly feeling the loss. Leaving my therapy appointment, I felt worse because it was the first time I truly faced the events that transpired just a week ago.

I wanted to end this book with a happy and optimistic tone, one of hope and belief that everything will be okay. I am struggling to write that message right now. Such is grief and learning to live with the loss of a child. There are good days and bad, and usually, the worst days are closest to the actual events happening, and sometimes they're not. Sometimes they're days, weeks, or months away after being triggered by a memory—an ultrasound photo, a gift for your child that they will never receive.

We are a week away from receiving results of genetic testing of our baby and also additional genetic testing that Kevin and I underwent last week. A week away from hopefully receiving some answers, but nothing is certain. The unfortunate piece of this whole scenario is that neither outcome feels positive. If a chromosome abnormality is detected, then we have a long road ahead of us to explore IVF, and that is not something I am confident I can do. The short online search I was able to complete last week before quickly shutting down our laptop spoke of daily shots at home, specific scheduling, freezing eggs...It was all too much to even try to comprehend. And this would be the "good" news. This would be the news that would set us on our next path and a whole new experience.

I can't help but wonder what next if nothing is found? Am I supposed to believe that our first three losses were due to my septate uterus and this last one just happened to fall within the typical 10–20 percent miscarriage rate? That is a real possibility that we face, and I am not sure how I would feel about that scenario. I am left with nothing but the question of how I will proceed. Will I rise from this with a renewed strength, or will I wallow and sink back into the darkness of my depression? Right now, on literal rainy days like today, it feels like the latter. It is just after 2:00 p.m.; and I want to take a hot shower, put on fresh sweats, and have a cold beer. I am fighting those feelings of restlessness, not wanting to be around anyone or really do anything.

I consider yesterday to be a massive success. I left the house for the first time by myself since last week, had an hour therapy session, and went grocery shopping. Food and cooking have always been somewhat therapeutic for me. I find it is the only time I am able to compartmentalize my feelings, in that I am only focused on the task at hand, whatever dish it is that I am making. The fact that I had the desire to meal plan for the rest of the week and weekend was a glimmer of hope. I know this to be true of myself, because when I am at my lowest of the lows, cooking is the furthest thing from my mind. Having this desire yesterday was a bit of a relief, and it also occupied several hours of being out of the house, making a meal plan on the road, and then visiting several stores to get all of the ingredients needed. I am more aware of my use of food as comfort, and it was surely apparent from the multitude of ice cream, cookies, and snacks that filled my carriage. This shopping trip was surely a departure from the health-crazed ones from the past, but I didn't care, I needed the comfort food.

Maybe that's just it, as I had this epiphany in writing earlier, maybe it is just finding something small that can bring some joy or some relief. I know that my happiness is my responsibility, and I am making active choices for how to view the world. Right now, I need to allow myself to feel the sadness in my heart, because there is no denying that it is there, and there to stay for some time. I have to remember my past losses and let them be a lesson for myself on how to pick me back up and choose to live another day, not just exist. I have to find gratitude for the things in my life that are blessings. I have to think of Kevin. I don't know where I would be without him. I am so grateful to call him my husband and that these experiences have brought us even closer than we were. I am grateful for my health, and my body, even when it doesn't do what I want it to. I am grateful for the peace that still lives in my heart beside the sadness.

As much as I want to question my will to continue down this path, I know that is just my current anger and sadness taking the reins of my thoughts. I know it is also my despair and not wanting to experience this ever again, a fear we will face with any future pregnancies. I know that there will be no greater blessing than the moment when Kevin and I welcome a child to our family, and so I know that I will find the strength to continue on, because I know that all this pain will be worth it. I can only imagine the love I will feel when I meet my child face-to-face because I have felt that love so strongly in my dreams that I can't imagine what the real thing is like. I know I will keep trying because I know the greatest joy of my marriage will be to see Kevin as a father. I know I will keep trying because I do believe I was meant to be a mother, even if I still can't picture it for myself.

Today is February 26, and I haven't written in weeks. I have been too consumed by my grief to do much else other than try to survive. I have isolated myself and began self-medicating again. Clearly, there is a cycle I have established to move through our losses. I am much more self-aware this time around though, and I'm grateful that through these experiences I can see the personal growth that I have achieved. I am grateful that I have my writing to read. It's a reminder that I've been here before and have made it through to the other side.

There is still a long way to go, but I need to celebrate how far I have come. I also have to accept that my emotions come in cycles and that right now I am grieving and it's okay.

Kevin and I spoke about taking a break from trying this week. We both got hit hard with the flu, and the toll it took on our mental health was unexpected. We were horizontal for what seemed like an eternity but, in fact, was closer to a week. This time of slowing down forced me to reflect on our journey this last year and a half trying to conceive, and I felt I had an epiphany, a new understanding of my character traits I am already aware of. The best way to explain it is this feeling of finally getting off of a Ferris wheel you didn't know you were on. We've been so laser focused on starting our family and continuing down this path regardless of where it took us that we never really stopped and looked around.

Each new event and piece of information was absorbed only to make the next decision. We've been on a marathon, and I feel like my body is finally shutting down and saying, "Enough." Looking back, I've been pregnant every few months, only giving myself a few months break in between each loss because we had to physically or because I gave myself a little time to mentally prepare. This time around is different because I realize that by staying on this course so rigidly that I am not giving myself the mental and physical break from this process that I now need. The physical and mental recovery of our last loss is making me feel that the choice is not mine. It is being made for me. I am finally listening to the natural flow of my life. I need to think about living my life with my husband and not counting weeks or mapping my ovulation. I need to focus on the little things in my life that can still bring me joy as I battle the sadness from our last lost child.

In the last few weeks, we have received more information on our testing results. Our baby's results came back as an "abnormal male," who suffered from Down syndrome. Dr. Grow confirmed for us that this abnormality is what caused me to miscarry. I felt immediately defensive of my child upon hearing this news. I was anticipating what people might say or how they would respond upon hearing the news. And I didn't want to face anyone telling me our loss was for the best or something else of that nature. I was of course saddened to learn this news but was at least grateful to have a "root cause" to answer my never-ending questions of "Why?" This was a new concern I now have, that if we were lucky enough to carry full term, that our child would be born with a life-altering disability. It just felt so unfair to think about after all we had already been through.

Then we received our independent genetic panel results where I tested positive as a potential carrier for spinal muscular atrophy, where if Kevin was also a carrier, our child could face death at six months of age for the most severe cases or have motor skills impacted as a teen or adult for milder cases. Luckily, Kevin's results came back negative, and so now we at least have our path defined a bit more, knowing that for now IVF is not in our future.

As much as I have convinced myself that I am learning to go with the flow, letting go of my need to control, the reality is that I still have a very long way to go. In fact, I believe surrendering is my life lesson. As much as I know I have grown, I am now taking a big step back and seeing there is still much work to do. I thought I was starting to let go, but I've still been so laser focused on getting pregnant that it's hard to see much else when looking back on the last eighteen months, and that thought in itself is a bit sobering, to know how I've been living my life with blinders on to everything not baby related.

I know that my growth and grief will come in ebbs and flows. I know that I will never truly get over my losses, and quite frankly, I don't want to. My babies have changed me, and the woman that I am becoming. When I think of becoming a mother, I am filled with feelings of fear. I have adverse reactions to things that would excite joy in women that have never experienced a loss, and that is okay. I have to honor myself and where I am. I have to allow myself the time I need to move through these cycles. The thing I am most grateful for now is that while I know the darkest of days, I know they always come to light. Reading through these pages is a timeline in a way for me, a reminder for the waves of emotions I feel as I experienced these very real-life experiences. It is reassuring to me to reread about the depths of my despair from my previous losses because I know I got through them to the other side—and I know I will again.

As I read through these pages again, it seems to provide new insights for me, new insights about myself and the events that have transpired. Revisiting the cards that were drawn for me during that fateful reiki session have new meaning for me now.

1. I am ready, thank you.
2. I am the weaver of my reality.
3. I forgive and let go with loving ease.
4. I am courageous, steady, and strong.
5. My emotions move through cycles and connect me to my truth.
6. I unleash my wildness and choose to be free.
7. My inner compass knows the way

The one that keeps rising to the surface is *My emotions move through cycles and connect me to my truth*. It is almost as if my initial interpretation of the meanings are no longer relevant, and these new realizations and understandings are now reinforced tenfold. It is as if I am seeing them with new eyes, or maybe it is my new perspective, either way it feels like an epiphany and I am grateful for this new view.

For now, I am going to get back to living my life, loving my husband, and doing small things that can bring me joy to balance out the despair. Each day gets a tiny bit easier, and I am holding on to that. I am also holding on to the hope that we will try to start a family again, maybe later this year, maybe next year, but only when we feel ready and only after allowing ourselves the much-needed time to recharge. In the meantime, I am going to do my best to live by this quote: "You can still know peace without knowing what comes next" (@morganharpernichols). And my hope is that you can try to do the same.

About the Author

Lorraine Frederick is a first-time author who currently lives in her hometown of Meriden, Connecticut. When she's not busy writing, her full-time focus is her non-profit public charity she cofounded with her husband, Social Sabby, which focuses on support and inclusion of special needs children. In earlier years she's been a director of marketing and lived in New York City while working in the fashion industry. Lorraine has always enjoyed writing, but it wasn't until her experience trying to conceive that she considered pursuing it professionally to share her tumultuous story with others. Her hope is that this book will be a resource to other grieving mothers to help provide them with support during their moments of despair, while also helping to start the important conversation to remove the stigma surrounding pregnancy loss. As this book went into production, Lorraine and her husband experienced their fifth loss and received the recommendation to move forward with in vitro fertilization as their next step. She hopes to continue documenting her journey trying to conceive and sharing her story with those walking a similar path.

CPSIA information can be obtained
at www.ICGtesting.com
Printed in the USA
BVHW081127090321
602109BV00008B/80

9 781644 688724